YOUTH EDITION

STEPS TO CHRIST

E. G. WHITE

REVIEW AND HERALD® PUBLISHING ASSOCIATION
Since 1861 | www.reviewandherald.com

This book was edited by Gary B. Swanson
Cover design by Ron Pride
Interior design by Glen Milam

Printed by Pacific Press® Publishing Association
Printed in U.S.A.

ISBN 978-0-8280-2093-0

April 2021

To accurately convey the nineteenth-century intent of the author, wherever the word "intercourse" originally appeared in this book, it has been replaced with the word "relationship."

ACKNOWLEDGEMENTS

Ellen White, the author of *Steps to Christ*, was a woman of remarkable spiritual gifts who lived most of her life during the nineteenth century. Through her writing and ministry she has made a revolutionary impact on millions of people around the world.

During her lifetime she wrote more than 5,000 periodical articles and 26 books. She is the most translated woman writer in the history of literature, and the most translated American author of either gender. Her writings cover a broad range of subjects, including religion, education, health, social relationships, evangelism, prophecy, publishing, nutrition, and management. *Steps to Christ* has been published in more than 135 languages.

The following people contributed to the writing of the devotional sidebars that are intended to amplify and illustrate the text of *Steps to Christ* in this special, centennial edition for youth: Karen Blumenberg, Loree Chase, Peter Chiomenti, Bill Cleveland, Curt Dewees, Vikki Fields, Randy Fishell, Carol Ann Fraser, Cheryl Holloway, Beverly Kelly, Gary Krause, Janya Mekelburg, Luan Miller, Shelly Nolan, Lori Peckham, Keith Potts, Gary Swanson, Jerry Thomas, and Sergio Torres. The contributions of each of these writers is signified by his or her initials at the end of each devotional sidebar.

Presented to:

____

By:

____

Message:

____

____

____

____

____

GOD'S LOVE FOR MAN

Nature and revelation alike testify of God's love. Our Father in heaven is the source of life, of wisdom, and of joy. Look at the wonderful and beautiful things of nature. Think of their marvelous adaptation to the needs and happiness, not only of man, but of all living creatures. The sunshine and the rain, that gladden and refresh the earth, the hills and seas and plains, all speak to us of the Creator's love. It is God who supplies the daily needs of all His creatures. In the beautiful words of the psalmist—

"The eyes of all wait upon Thee;
And Thou givest them their meat in due season.
Thou openest Thine hand,
And satisfiest the desire of every living thing."
Psalm 145:15, 16.

God made man perfectly holy and happy; and the fair earth, as it came from the Creator's hand, bore no blight of decay or shadow of the curse. It is transgression of God's law—the law of love—that has brought woe and death. Yet even amid the suffering that results from sin, God's love is revealed. It is written that God cursed the ground for man's sake. Genesis 3:17. The thorn and the thistle—the difficulties and trials that make his life one of toil and care—were appointed for his good as a part of the training needful in

Jesus did not suppress one word of truth, but He uttered it always in love.

God's plan for his uplifting from the ruin and degradation that sin has wrought. The world, though fallen, is not all sorrow and misery. In nature itself are messages of hope and comfort. There are flowers upon the thistles, and the thorns are covered with roses.

(1) "God is love" is written upon every opening bud, upon every spire of springing grass. The lovely birds making the air

N A T U R E

THE SWEET AND THE INNOCENT

In the lush rain forests of Costa Rica, competition for sunlight is fierce. When an aging giant falls, seedlings race to fill the gap in the canopy, and vines cling to the seedlings for a ride up into the sun. But one young tree is always free of unwanted hitchhikers.

Each swollen thorn acacia seedling hosts a colony of ants that act as guardians. The ants cut off the leaves of encroaching vines, and sting visiting insects that would find the acacia leaves a tasty meal, allowing the acacia to grow toward the sun in peace.

In turn the ants live in the acacia's large hollow thorns, drink the sweet nectar that exudes from the base of the leaf stems, and feed their larvae with special protein-rich structures that grow at the tip of some of the leaves. It's a happy situation for both the ant colony and the tree.

What great fun God must have had, working out all the living arrangements that ensure each living thing "a place in the sun." The indicated paragraph (see (1) on page 6) shows how nature shows God's love.

- How does this cooperation between the acacias and ants declare that "God is love"?
- What is there about your life that says to the world, "God is love"?

CONSIDER...

- looking around you for something that God made. What might God be saying to you through His work?
- recalling the words to "This is my Father's World." Sing them to yourself as you take a walk.

FOR MORE, SEE...

- Psalm 65:11-13
- Isaiah 61:11
- Romans 1:20

—CH

vocal with their happy songs, the delicately tinted flowers in their perfection perfuming the air, the lofty trees of the forest with their rich foliage of living green—all testify to the tender, fatherly care of our God and to His desire to make His children happy.

The word of God reveals His character. He Himself has declared His infinite love and pity. When Moses prayed, "Show me Thy glory," the Lord answered, "I will make all My goodness pass before thee." Exodus 33:18, 19. This is His glory. The Lord passed before Moses, and proclaimed, "The Lord, The Lord God, merciful and gracious, long-suffering, and abundant in goodness and truth, keeping mercy for thousands, forgiving iniquity and transgression and sin." Exodus 34:6, 7. He is "slow to anger, and of great kindness," "because He delighteth in mercy." Jonah 4:2; Micah 7:18.

In nature itself are messages of hope and comfort. There are flowers upon the thistles, and the thorns are covered with roses.

God has bound our hearts to Him by unnumbered tokens in heaven and in earth. Through the things of nature, and the deepest and tenderest earthly ties that human hearts can know, He has sought to reveal Himself to us. Yet these but imperfectly represent His love. Though all these evidences have been given, the enemy of good blinded the minds of men, so that they looked upon God with fear; they thought of Him as severe and unforgiving. Satan led men to conceive of God as a being whose chief attribute is stern justice,—one who is a severe judge, a harsh, exacting creditor. He pictured the Creator as a being who is watching with jealous eye to discern the errors and mistakes of men, that He may visit judgments upon them. It was to remove this dark shadow, by revealing to the world the infinite love of God, that Jesus came to live among men.

The Son of God came from heaven to make manifest the Father. "No man hath seen God at any time; the only begotten Son, which is in the bosom of the Father, He hath declared Him." John 1:18. "Neither knoweth any man the Father, save the Son, and he to whomsoever the Son will reveal Him." Matthew 11:27. When one of the disciples made the request, "Show us the Father," Jesus answered, "Have I been so long time with you, and yet hast thou not known Me, Philip? He that hath seen Me hath seen the Father; and how sayest thou then, Show us the Father?" John 14:8, 9.

In describing His earthly mission, Jesus said, The Lord "hath anointed Me to preach the gospel to the poor; He hath sent Me to heal the brokenhearted, to preach deliverance to the captives, and recovering of sight to the blind, to set at liberty them that are bruised." Luke 4:18. This was His work. He went about doing good and healing all that were oppressed by Satan. There were whole villages where there was not a moan of sickness in any house, for He had passed through them and healed all their sick. His work gave evidence of His divine anointing. Love, mercy, and compassion were revealed in every act of His life; His heart went out in tender sympathy to the children of men. He took man's nature, that He might reach man's wants. The poorest and humblest were not afraid to approach Him. Even little children were attracted to Him. They loved to climb upon His knees and gaze into the pensive face, benignant with love.

(2) Jesus did not suppress one word of truth, but He uttered it always in love. He exercised the greatest tact and thoughtful, kind attention in His relationships with the people. He was never rude, never needlessly spoke a severe word, never gave needless pain to a sensitive soul. He did not censure human weakness. He

spoke the truth, but always in love. He denounced hypocrisy, unbelief, and iniquity; but tears were in His voice as He uttered His scathing rebukes. He wept over Jerusalem, the city He loved, which refused to receive Him, the way, the truth, and the life. They had rejected Him, the Saviour, but He regarded them with pitying tenderness. His life was one of self-denial and thoughtful care for others. Every soul was precious in His eyes. While He ever bore

G O D ' S   L O V E

UNSPOKEN LOVE

"I love you." A phrase foreign to Derek. At least, those magic words had never slipped through the lips of the person he desperately longed to hear them from—Dad.

In the middle of a bitter December night, Derek suddenly awoke and sat bolt upright. Adrenalin surged through his body. It had been a dream, a bad one. In it Dad had died.

Spinning out of bed, Derek moved quickly across the hall and into his dad's room. He gently awakened his father. As Dad shook the sleep from his system, Derek blurted out, "Dad, I have to know. Do you love me?"

Silence. Tears fell from Dad's eyes. He then drew Derek close and embraced him. Still no words, but it was enough. The magic had happened.

God's love for you is always there. No spoken words. Just a cross. The indicated paragraph (see ☛2 on page 8) will tell you more about God's love.

- Why are the promises of God's love hard for some to grasp?
- Looking around, what evidences of God's love do you see right now?

CONSIDER...

- showing Mom or Dad or your sister or brother that you love him or her. Bake something or clean up a messy room—yours or someone else's.
- asking God to help you take hold of another's unspoken love for you.

FOR MORE, SEE...

- Zephaniah 3:17
- John 3:16, 17
- John 15:13

—RF

Himself with divine dignity, He bowed with the tenderest regard to every member of the family of God. In all men He saw fallen souls whom it was His mission to save.

Such is the character of Christ as revealed in His life. This is the character of God. It is from the Father's heart that the streams of divine compassion, manifest in Christ, flow out to the children of men. Jesus, the tender, pitying Saviour, was God "manifest in the flesh." 1 Timothy 3:16.

It was to redeem us that Jesus lived and suffered and died. He became "a Man of Sorrows," that we might be made partakers of everlasting joy. God permitted His beloved Son, full of grace and truth, to come from a world of indescribable glory, to a world marred and blighted with sin, darkened with the shadow of death and the curse. He permitted Him to leave the bosom of His love, the adoration of the angels, to suffer shame, insult, humiliation, hatred, and death. "The chastisement of our peace was upon Him; and with His stripes we are healed." Isaiah 53:5. Behold Him in the wilderness, in Gethsemane, upon the cross! The spotless Son of God took upon Himself the burden of sin. He who had been one with God, felt in His soul the awful separation that sin makes between God and man. This wrung from His lips the anguished cry, "My God, My God, why hast Thou forsaken Me?" Matthew 27:46. It was the burden of sin, the sense of its terrible enormity, of its separation of the soul from God—it was this that broke the heart of the Son of God.

But this great sacrifice was not made in order to create in the Father's heart a love for man, not to make Him willing to save. No, no! "God so loved the world, that He gave His only-begotten Son." John 3:16. The Father loves us, not because of the great propitiation, but He provided the propitiation because He loves us. Christ was the medium through which He could pour out His infinite love upon a fallen world. "God was in Christ, reconciling the world unto Himself." 2 Corinthians 5:19. God suffered with His Son. In the agony of Gethsemane, the death of Calvary, the heart of Infinite Love paid the price of our redemption.

Jesus said, "Therefore doth My Father love Me, because I lay down My life, that I might take it again." John 10:17. That is, "My Father has so loved you that He even loves Me more for giving My life to redeem you. In becoming your Substitute and Surety, by surrendering My life, by taking your liabilities, your transgressions, I am endeared to My Father; for by My sacrifice, God can be just, and yet the Justifier of him who believeth in Jesus."

Nothing less than the infinite sacrifice made by Christ in behalf of fallen man could express the Father's love to lost humanity.

None but the Son of God could accomplish our redemption; for only He who was in the bosom of the Father could declare Him. Only He who knew the height and depth of the love of God could make it manifest. Nothing less than the infinite sacrifice made by Christ in behalf of fallen man could express the Father's love to lost humanity.

"God so loved the world, that He gave His only-begotten Son." He gave Him not only to live among men, to bear their sins, and die their sacrifice. He gave Him to the fallen race. Christ was to identify Himself with the interests and needs of humanity. He who was one with God has linked Himself with the children of men by ties that are never to be broken. Jesus is "not ashamed to call them brethren" (Hebrews 2:11); He is our Sacrifice, our Advocate, our Brother, bearing our human form before the Father's throne, and through eternal ages one with the race He has redeemed—the Son of man. And all this that man might be uplifted from the ruin and degradation of sin that he might reflect the love of God and share the joy of holiness.

(3) The price paid for our redemption, the infinite sacrifice of our heavenly Father in giving His Son to die for us, should give us exalted conceptions of what we may become through Christ. As the inspired apostle John beheld the height, the depth, the breadth of the Father's love toward the perishing race, he was filled with

S E L F - E S T E E M

IN BIG TROUBLE

In 1991 the city of Philadelphia discovered that for two years it had had no enforcement program for traffic tickets. Seventy-five percent of those who'd received traffic citations had ignored them. So officials sent out a list of names to be arrested. At the top of the list was Richard Canning.

Canning had racked up 301 moving violations in two years: seven for careless driving, 15 for disregarding traffic lights and stop signs, 52 for driving an uninspected vehicle, 58 for driving without registration, and 85 for driving without a license. "Lesser" violations included littering on the highway, driving without headlights, driving with a defective muffler, and others. Richard Canning faced an 85-year suspension of his license and $59,585 in fines.

He must have felt a lot like you may feel when you think about sin in your life. Satan likes to discourage you about your efforts to stop sinning. But Jesus thinks you're pretty special. You are a child of God. The indicated paragraph (see (3) on page 12) will give you some idea of how important you are.

- What could you tell Richard Canning about Jesus' love that would make him feel better about himself?
- What does being a child of God mean to you?

CONSIDER...

- reviewing the words of the familiar song, "Jesus Loves Me." How do they make you feel about yourself?
- observing a group of children at play. Think about what childlike qualities you would like to develop to grow closer to your Heavenly Father.

FOR MORE, SEE...

- Psalm 8
- Romans 5:6-8
- 1 Timothy 4:12

—*GS*

adoration and reverence; and, failing to find suitable language in which to express the greatness and tenderness of this love, he called upon the world to behold it. "Behold, what manner of love the Father hath bestowed upon us, that we should be called the sons of God." 1 John 3:1. What a value this places upon man! Through transgression the sons of man become subjects of Satan. Through faith in the atoning sacrifice of Christ the sons of Adam may become the sons of God. By assuming human nature, Christ elevates humanity. Fallen men are placed where, through connection with Christ, they may indeed become worthy of the name "sons of God."

Such love is without a parallel. Children of the heavenly King! Precious promise! Theme for the most profound meditation! The matchless love of God for a world that did not love Him! The thought has a subduing power upon the soul and brings the mind into captivity to the will of God. The more we study the divine character in the light of the cross, the more we see mercy, tenderness, and forgiveness blended with equity and justice, and the more clearly we discern innumerable evidences of a love that is infinite and a tender pity surpassing a mother's yearning sympathy for her wayward child.

THE SINNER'S NEED OF CHRIST

Man was originally endowed with noble powers and a well-balanced mind. He was perfect in his being, and in harmony with God. His thoughts were pure, his aims holy. But through disobedience, his powers were perverted, and selfishness took the place of love. His nature became so weakened through transgression that it was impossible for him, in his own strength, to resist the power of evil. He was made captive by Satan, and would have remained so forever had not God specially interposed. It was the tempter's purpose to thwart the divine plan in man's creation, and fill the earth with woe and desolation. And he would point to all this evil as the result of God's work in creating man.

In his sinless state, man held joyful communion with Him "in whom are hid all the treasures of wisdom and knowledge." Colossians 2:3. But after his sin, he could no longer find joy in holiness, and he sought to hide from the presence of God. Such is still the condition of the unrenewed heart. It is not in harmony with God, and finds no joy in communion with Him. The sinner could not be happy in God's presence; he would shrink from the companionship of holy beings. Could he be permitted to enter heaven, it would have no joy for him. The spirit of unselfish love that reigns there—every heart responding to the heart of Infinite Love—would touch no answering chord in his soul. His thoughts, his interests, his motives, would be alien to those that actuate the sinless dwellers there. He would be a discordant note in the melody of heaven. Heaven would be to him a place of torture; he would long to be hidden from Him who is its light, and the center of its joy. It is no arbitrary decree on the part of God that excludes the wicked from heaven; they are shut out by their own unfitness for its companionship. The glory of God would be to them a consuming fire. They would welcome destruction, that they might be hidden from the face of Him who died to redeem them.

It is impossible for us, of ourselves, to escape from the pit of sin in which we are sunken. Our hearts are evil, and we cannot

S I N F U L N E S S

HOW GREAT AM I?

One day Canute, an eleventh-century Danish king of England, grew so tired of his courtier's flattery that he ordered his chair be taken to the seashore. There, before them all, he commanded the waves not to get him wet. Soon the advancing tide lapped over his feet and proved the worth of human commands–even those of kings.

It's easy to view your life with self-satisfaction and to forget where your blessings come from. Scoring the game-winning goal, making the highest score on a chemistry test, getting a date with the prettiest girl in the class, owning the latest model of car—all are things that can give a false sense of value.

From the time of Canute's demonstration at the seashore, he never again wore his crown. Instead he placed it upon the head of a statue of the crucified Christ. Though he was a powerful king, Canute knew that next to Jesus' example, he was a sinner, just like the rest of humanity. The indicated paragraph (see (4) on page 14) shows how humanity's goodness compares to that of God.

- How does Canute's action illustrate the idea that a sinner is "a discordant note in the melody of heaven"?
- In what ways is it sometimes tempting to lose perspective about your accomplishments?

CONSIDER...

- listing six ways that sinfulness has affected the natural surroundings where you live.
- looking through magazines or newspapers for examples of the effects of sinfulness in the lives of others.

FOR MORE, SEE...

- Genesis 3:1-13, 16-24
- Romans 6:23
- Colossians 2:3

—GS

change them. "Who can bring a clean thing out of an unclean? not one." "The carnal mind is enmity against God: for it is not subject to the law of God, neither indeed can be." Job 14:4; Romans 8:7. Education, culture, the exercise of the will, human effort, all have their proper sphere, but here they are powerless. They may produce an outward correctness of behavior, but they cannot change the heart; they cannot purify the springs of life. There must be a power working from within, a new life from above, before men can be changed from sin to holiness. That power is Christ. His grace alone can quicken the lifeless faculties of the soul, and attract it to God, to holiness.

It is impossible for us, of ourselves, to escape from the pit of sin in which we are sunken.

The Saviour said, "Except a man be born from above," unless he shall receive a new heart, new desires, purposes, and motives, leading to a new life, "he cannot see the kingdom of God." John 3:3, margin. The idea that it is necessary only to develop the good that exists in man by nature, is a fatal deception. "The natural man receiveth not the things of the Spirit of God: for they are foolishness unto him: neither can he know them, because they are spiritually discerned." "Marvel not that I said unto thee, Ye must be born again." 1 Corinthians 2:14; John 3:7. Of Christ it is written, "In Him was life; and the life was the light of men"—the only "name under heaven given among men, whereby we must be saved." John 1:4; Acts 4:12.

It is not enough to perceive the loving-kindness of God, to see the benevolence, the fatherly tenderness, of His character. It is not enough to discern the wisdom and justice of His law, to see that it is founded upon the eternal principle of love. Paul the apostle saw all this when he exclaimed, "I consent unto the law that it is good." "The law is holy, and the commandment holy, and just, and good." But he added, in the bitterness of his soul-anguish and despair, "I am carnal, sold under sin." Romans 7:16, 12, 14. He longed for the purity, the righteousness, to which in himself he was powerless to attain, and cried out, "O wretched man that I am! who shall deliver me from this body of death?" Romans 7:24,

G U I L T

ON A GUILT TRIP

After serving two prison terms for theft and forgery, Larry appeared to be driven by some inner compulsion to continue breaking the law. He went on another check-writing spree, even signing his own name to the checks. It was ridiculously easy to prove his guilt for a third prison term.

When Larry was serving his second term, he experienced a temporary release from guilt—he was being punished. But he did not feel fully forgiven. When he was released, that something within sentenced him to further punishment. When he signed his own name to the worthless checks, it was as though he were saying, "I am still guilty. Find me and punish me."

God has created you in such a way that your guilt must be resolved. You may feel ashamed, rejected, inferior, and worthless. No matter how you feel, however, Jesus' unconditional love and forgiveness are always available to you. The indicated paragraph (see (5) on page 18) will show you how Jacob learned to deal with his guilt.

- How was Larry's way of dealing with guilt different from the way in which Jacob dealt with it?
- How differently does God deal with your guilt compared to the way it is treated in criminals today?

CONSIDER...

- making a list of feelings you experience when you've done something wrong.
- interviewing a Christian lawyer or judge in your community. Ask him or her to explain the differences between God's system of justice and humanity's system of justice.

FOR MORE, SEE...

- Psalm 31:1-5
- Psalm 31:9-11
- Ephesians 1:7, 8

—ST

margin. Such is the cry that has gone up from burdened hearts in all lands and in all ages. To all, there is but one answer, "Behold the Lamb of God, which taketh away the sin of the world." John 1:29.

Many are the figures by which the Spirit of God has sought to illustrate this truth, and make it plain to souls that long to be freed from the burden of guilt. When, after his sin in deceiving Esau, Jacob fled from his father's home, he was weighed down with a sense of guilt. Lonely and outcast as he was, separated from all that had made life dear, the one thought that above all others pressed upon his soul, was the fear that his sin had cut him off from God, that he was forsaken of Heaven. In sadness he lay down to rest on the bare earth, around him only the lonely hills, and above, the heavens bright with stars. As he slept, a strange light broke upon his vision; and lo, from the plain on which he lay, vast shadowy stairs seemed to lead upward to the very gates of heaven, and upon them angels of God were passing up and down; while from the glory above, the divine voice was heard in a message of comfort and hope. Thus was made known to Jacob that which met the need and longing of his soul—a Saviour. With joy and gratitude he saw revealed a way by which he, a sinner, could be restored to communion with God. The mystic ladder of his dream represented Jesus, the only medium of communication between God and man.

This is the same figure to which Christ referred in His conversation with Nathanael, when He said, "Ye shall see heaven open, and the angels of God ascending and descending upon the Son of man." John 1:51. In the apostasy, man alienated himself from God; earth was cut off from heaven. Across the gulf that lay between, there could be no communion. But through Christ, earth is again linked with heaven. With His own merits, Christ has bridged the gulf which sin had made, so that the ministering angels can hold communion with man. Christ connects fallen man in his weakness and helplessness with the Source of infinite power.

(6) But in vain are men's dreams of progress, in vain all efforts for the uplifting of humanity, if they neglect the one Source of hope and help for the fallen race. "Every good gift and every perfect gift" (James 1:17) is from God. There is no true excellence

HUMAN PROGRESS

WATERLOGGED LOGGING

The destruction of South American rain forests has many people worried that modern progress has gone too far. We're destroying the only planet we have. But one businessman is turning destruction into a unique opportunity.

With thousands of miles of rain forest underwater from the construction of a hydroelectric dam in Para, Brazil, Juarez Christiano Gomes came up with the idea of underwater logging. He even invented electric saws that work underwater. Lumberjacks—wearing air tanks—go down as far as 164 feet to cut the wood. Instead of having to watch for falling timber they have to look out for trees floating up to the surface, where they are towed to a sawmill.

God gave us this earth to care for, and we haven't always done such a good job of it. Sometimes our progress only takes us backward. But God can make anything good. Even us.

God has given us "every good and perfect gift," (James 1:17, NIV). All we have to do is accept. The indicated paragraph (see (6) on page 19) suggests that God is the only One who can make us good.

- What are the chances for true progress if we leave God out of the picture?
- What does God offer us that is better than anything available in the world today?

CONSIDER...

- reading a book on the environment and on humanity's attempts to save it.
- writing God a poem, song, or personal letter in appreciation for what He has done for you personally.

FOR MORE, SEE...

- Genesis 11:1-8
- Philippians 4:8
- Revelation 21:1-4

—LM

of character apart from Him. And the only way to God is Christ. He says, "I am the way, the truth, and the life: no man cometh unto the Father, but by Me." John 14:6.

The heart of God yearns over His earthly children with a love stronger than death. In giving up His Son, He has poured out to us all heaven in one gift. The Saviour's life and death and intercession, the ministry of angels, the pleading of the Spirit, the Father working above and through all, the unceasing interest of heavenly beings,—all are enlisted in behalf of man's redemption.

Oh, let us contemplate the amazing sacrifice that has been made for us! Let us try to appreciate the labor and energy that Heaven is expending to reclaim the lost, and bring them back to the Father's house. Motives stronger, and agencies more powerful, could never be brought into operation; the exceeding rewards for right-doing, the enjoyment of heaven, the society of the angels, the communion and love of God and His Son, the elevation and extension of all our powers throughout eternal ages—are these not mighty incentives and encouragements to urge us to give the heart's loving service to our Creator and Redeemer?

And, on the other hand, the judgments of God pronounced against sin, the inevitable retribution, the degradation of our character, and the final destruction, are presented in God's word to warn us against the service of Satan.

Shall we not regard the mercy of God? What more could He do? Let us place ourselves in right relation to Him who has loved us with amazing love. Let us avail ourselves of the means provided for us that we may be transformed into His likeness, and be restored to fellowship with the ministering angels, to harmony and communion with the Father and the Son.

REPENTANCE

How shall a man be just with God? How shall the sinner be made righteous? It is only through Christ that we can be brought into harmony with God, with holiness; but how are we to come to Christ? Many are asking the same question as did the multitude on the Day of Pentecost, when, convicted of sin, they cried out, "What shall we do?" The first word of Peter's answer was, "Repent." Acts 2:37, 38. At another time, shortly after, he said, "Repent, . . . and be converted, that your sins may be blotted out." Acts 3:19.

Repentance includes sorrow for sin and a turning away from it. We shall not renounce sin unless we see its sinfulness; until we turn away from it in heart, there will be no real change in the life.

There are many who fail to understand the true nature of repentance. Multitudes sorrow that they have sinned and even make an outward reformation because they fear that their wrongdoing will bring suffering upon themselves. But this is not repentance in the Bible sense. They lament the suffering rather than the sin. Such was the grief of Esau when he saw that the birthright was lost to him forever. Balaam, terrified by the angel standing in his pathway with drawn sword, acknowledged his guilt lest he should lose his life; but there was no genuine repentance for sin, no conversion of purpose, no abhorrence of evil. Judas Iscariot, after betraying his Lord, exclaimed, "I have sinned in that I have betrayed the innocent blood." Matthew 27:4.

The confession was forced from his guilty soul by an awful sense of condemnation and a fearful looking for of judgment. The consequences that were to result to him filled him with terror, but there was no deep, heartbreaking grief in his soul, that he had betrayed the spotless Son of God and denied the Holy One of Israel. Pharaoh, when suffering under the judgments of God, acknowledged his sin in order to escape further punishment, but returned to his defiance of Heaven as soon as the plagues were stayed. These all lamented the results of sin, but did not sorrow for the sin itself.

But when the heart yields to the influence of the Spirit of God, the conscience will be quickened, and the sinner will discern something of the depth and sacredness of God's holy law, the foundation of His government in heaven and on earth. The "Light, which lighteth every man that cometh into the world," illumines the secret chambers of the soul, and the hidden things of darkness are made manifest. John 1:9. Conviction takes hold upon the mind and heart. The sinner has a sense of the righteousness of Jehovah and feels the terror of appearing, in his own guilt and uncleanness, before the Searcher of hearts. He sees the love of God, the beauty of holiness, the joy of purity; he longs to be cleansed and to be restored to communion with Heaven.

[7] The prayer of David after his fall, illustrates the nature of true sorrow for sin. His repentance was sincere and deep. There was no effort to palliate his guilt; no desire to escape the judgment threatened, inspired his prayer. David saw the enormity of his transgression; he saw the defilement of his soul; he loathed his sin. It was not for pardon only that he prayed, but for purity of heart. He longed for the joy of holiness—to be restored to harmony and communion with God. This was the language of his soul:

> "Blessed is he whose transgression is forgiven, whose sin is covered.
> Blessed is the man unto whom the Lord imputeth not iniquity,
> And in whose spirit there is no guile."
>
> Psalm 32:1, 2.

"Have mercy upon me, O God, according to Thy loving-kindness:
According unto the multitude of Thy tender mercies blot out my transgressions. . . .
For I acknowledge my transgressions: and my sin is ever before me. . . .
Purge me with hyssop, and I shall be clean: wash me, and I shall be whiter than snow. . . .

R E P E N T A N C E

DYING FOR FORGIVENESS

A few years ago a woman tried to kill her husband. Five times! She put ground glass in his drink. She put rat poison in his food. She put a black widow spider in his bed. She hit him on the head with a hammer while he was sleeping. She hired some friends to shoot him. Nothing worked.

Finally the wife wept and asked her husband to forgive her. He responded, "I still love you and I forgive you. I want us to go back together as husband and wife."

When we ask God to forgive us, whatever we have done, He responds by telling us, "I still love you." He releases us from the prison of our heavy conscience. He brings us back into His world, into His family, into His heart. He treats us as if we had never done anything bad to Him. The indicated paragraph (see 7 on page 22) will show how bad David felt about his sins and what happened when he came to God for forgiveness.

- Do you feel that the wife had done too much to her husband for him to forgive her?
- Should we continue to feel bad about our sins after we have asked God to forgive us?

CONSIDER...

- making a list of things in your life that make Jesus sad and determining to ask His forgiveness.
- forgiving someone of something that he or she has done to you, even if he or she does not ask for forgiveness.

FOR MORE, SEE...

- Matthew 11:28
- Romans 2:4
- Romans 5:6-8

—BC

Create in me a clean heart, O God;
And renew a right spirit within me.
Cast me not away from Thy presence;
And take not Thy Holy Spirit from me.
Restore unto me the joy of Thy salvation;
And uphold me with Thy free spirit. . . .
Deliver me from bloodguiltiness, O God, Thou God of my salvation:
And my tongue shall sing aloud of Thy righteousness."
Psalm 51:1-14.

A repentance such as this, is beyond the reach of our own power to accomplish; it is obtained only from Christ, who ascended up on high and has given gifts unto men.

Just here is a point on which many may err, and hence they fail of receiving the help that Christ desires to give them. They think that they cannot come to Christ unless they first repent, and that repentance prepares for the forgiveness of their sins. It is true that repentance does precede the forgiveness of sins; for it is only the broken and contrite heart that will feel the need of a Saviour. But must the sinner wait till he has repented before he can come to Jesus? Is repentance to be made an obstacle between the sinner and the Saviour?

The Bible does not teach that the sinner must repent before he can heed the invitation of Christ.

The Bible does not teach that the sinner must repent before he can heed the invitation of Christ, "Come unto Me, all ye that labor and are heavyladen, and I will give you rest." Matthew 11:28. It is the virtue that goes forth from Christ, that leads to genuine repentance. Peter made the matter clear in his statement to the Israelites when he said, "Him hath God exalted with His right hand to be a Prince and a Saviour, for to give repentance to Israel, and forgiveness of sins." Acts 5:31. We can no more repent without the Spirit of Christ to awaken the conscience than we can be pardoned without Christ.

Christ is the source of every right impulse. He is the only one that can implant in the heart enmity against sin. Every desire for truth and purity, every conviction of our own sinfulness, is an evidence that His Spirit is moving upon our hearts.

Jesus has said, "I, if I be lifted up from the earth, will draw all men unto Me." John 12:32. Christ must be revealed to the sinner as the Saviour dying for the sins of the world; and as we behold the Lamb of God upon the cross of Calvary, the mystery of redemption begins to unfold to our minds and the goodness of God leads us to repentance. In dying for sinners, Christ manifested a love that is incomprehensible; and as the sinner beholds this love, it softens the heart, impresses the mind, and inspires contrition in the soul.

It is true that men sometimes become ashamed of their sinful ways, and give up some of their evil habits, before they are conscious that they are being drawn to Christ. But whenever they make an effort to reform, from a sincere desire to do right, it is the power of Christ that is drawing them. An influence of which they are unconscious works upon the soul, and the conscience is quickened, and the outward life is amended. And as Christ draws them to look upon His cross, to behold Him whom their sins have pierced, the commandment comes home to the conscience. The wickedness of their life, the deep-seated sin of the soul, is revealed to them. They begin to comprehend something of the righteousness of Christ, and exclaim, "What is sin, that it should require such a sacrifice for the redemption of its victim? Was all this love, all this suffering, all this humiliation, demanded, that we might not perish, but have everlasting life?"

The sinner may resist this love, may refuse to be drawn to Christ; but if he does not resist he will be drawn to Jesus; a knowledge of the plan of salvation will lead him to the foot of the cross in repentance for his sins, which have caused the sufferings of God's dear Son.

The same divine mind that is working upon the things of nature is speaking to the hearts of men and creating an inexpressible craving for something they have not. The things of the world cannot satisfy their longing. The Spirit of God is pleading with them to seek for those things that alone can give peace and rest—the grace of Christ, the joy of holiness. Through influences seen and unseen, our Saviour is constantly at work to attract the minds of men from the unsatisfying pleasures of sin to the infinite blessings that may be theirs in Him. To all these souls, who are vainly seeking to drink from the broken cisterns of this world, the divine message is addressed, "Let him that is athirst come. And whosoever will, let him take the water of life freely." Revelation 22:17.

You who in heart long for something better than this world can give, recognize this longing as the voice of God to your soul. Ask Him to give you repentance, to reveal Christ to you in His infinite love, in His perfect purity. In the Saviour's life the principles of God's law—love to God and man—were perfectly exemplified. Benevolence, unselfish love, was the life of His soul. It is as we behold Him, as the light from our Saviour falls upon us, that we see the sinfulness of our own hearts.

8 We may have flattered ourselves, as did Nicodemus, that our life has been upright, that our moral character is correct, and think that we need not humble the heart before God, like the common sinner: but when the light from Christ shines into our

souls, we shall see how impure we are; we shall discern the selfishness of motive, the enmity against God, that has defiled every act of life. Then we shall know that our own righteousness is indeed as filthy rags, and that the blood of Christ alone can cleanse us from the defilement of sin, and renew our hearts in His own likeness.

One ray of the glory of God, one gleam of the purity of Christ, penetrating the soul, makes every spot of defilement

SELF-INSPECTION

THAT EERIE ACCUSATION

One author tells the story of a man who stood on a busy city street corner, quietly harassing people as they bustled by. From time to time the man would gravely point to the nearest person and loudly pronounce one word, "Guilty!" A few moments later he would single out another unfortunate victim, raise his arm mechanically, point, and again pronounce that dreaded word, "Guilty!"

The author says the effect on passing strangers was "extraordinary, almost eerie." People would stare, look away, avert their eyes, look at other people, and then hurry on. One of the accused victims responded by turning to someone and exclaiming, "But how did he know?"

Many people think that God acts like that man—always accusing us and pointing out our faults. But God doesn't work like that at all. This is what happens. He tries to reveal His love to us in many ways. As we start to see how wonderful He is, we also start to see how much we need Him. Read the indicated paragraph (see 8 on page 26) to see what we should do when we realize our faults.

- If God doesn't condemn us, what is His purpose for making us aware of our faults?
- Given the way God treats us, what should our attitude be to faults we see in other people?

CONSIDER...

- thanking God that He loves rather than condemns.
- writing 1 John 3:22 on a slip of paper and posting it where you will see it every day.

FOR MORE, SEE...

- John 3:16-21
- John 8:1-11
- 1 John 3:19-24

—GK

painfully distinct, and lays bare the deformity and defects of the human character. It makes apparent the unhallowed desires, the infidelity of the heart, the impurity of the lips. The sinner's acts of disloyalty in making void the law of God, are exposed to his sight, and his spirit is stricken and afflicted under the searching influence of the Spirit of God. He loathes himself as he views the pure, spotless character of Christ.

God does not regard all sins as of equal magnitude.

When the prophet Daniel beheld the glory surrounding the heavenly messenger that was sent unto him, he was overwhelmed with a sense of his own weakness and imperfection. Describing the effect of the wonderful scene, he says, "There remained no strength in me: for my comeliness was turned in me into corruption, and I retained no strength." Daniel 10:8. The soul thus touched will hate its selfishness, abhor its self-love, and will seek, through Christ's righteousness, for the purity of heart that is in harmony with the law of God and the character of Christ.

Paul says that as "touching the righteousness which is in the law"—as far as outward acts were concerned—he was "blameless" (Philippians 3:6); but when the spiritual character of the law was discerned, he saw himself a sinner. Judged by the letter of the law as men apply it to the outward life, he had abstained from sin; but when he looked into the depths of its holy precepts, and saw himself as God saw him, he bowed in humiliation and confessed his guilt. He says, "I was alive without the law once: but when the commandment came, sin revived, and I died." Romans 7:9. When he saw the spiritual nature of the law, sin appeared in its true hideousness, and his self-esteem was gone.

God does not regard all sins as of equal magnitude; there are degrees of guilt in His estimation, as well as in that of man; but however trifling this or that wrong act may seem in the eyes of men, no sin is small in the sight of God. Man's judgment is partial, imperfect; but God estimates all things as they really are. The drunkard is despised and is told that his sin will exclude him from heaven; while pride, selfishness, and covetousness too often go unrebuked. But these are sins that are especially offensive to God; for they are contrary to the benevolence of His character, to that unselfish love which is the very atmosphere of the unfallen universe. He who falls into some of the grosser sins may feel a sense of his shame and poverty and his need of the grace of Christ; but pride feels no need, and so it closes the heart against Christ and the infinite blessings He came to give.

The poor publican who prayed, "God be merciful to me a sinner" (Luke 18:13), regarded himself as a very wicked man, and others looked upon him in the same light; but he felt his need, and with his burden of guilt and shame he came before God, asking for His mercy. His heart was open for the Spirit of God to do its gracious work and set him free from the power of sin. The Pharisee's boastful, self-righteous prayer showed that his heart was closed against the influence of the Holy Spirit. Because of his distance from God, he had no sense of his own defilement, in contrast with the perfection of the divine holiness. He felt no need, and he received nothing.

If you see your sinfulness, do not wait to make yourself better. How many there are who think they are not good enough to come to Christ. Do you expect to become better through your own efforts? "Can the Ethiopian change his skin, or the leopard his spots? then may ye also do good, that are accustomed to do evil." Jeremiah 13:23. There is help for us only in God. We must not wait for stronger persuasions, for better opportunities, or for holier tempers. We can do nothing of ourselves. We must come to Christ just as we are.

But let none deceive themselves with the thought that God, in His great love and mercy, will yet save even the rejecters of His grace. The exceeding sinfulness of sin can be estimated only in the light of the cross. When men urge that God is too good to cast off the sinner, let them look to Calvary. It was because there was no other way in which man could be saved, because without this sacrifice it was impossible for the human race to escape from the defiling power of sin, and be restored to communion with holy beings,—impossible for them again to become partakers of spiritual life,—it was because of this that Christ took upon Himself the guilt of the disobedient and suffered in the sinner's stead. The love and suffering and death of the Son of God all testify to the terrible enormity of sin and declare that there is no escape from its power, no hope of the higher life, but through the submission of the soul to Christ.

The impenitent sometimes excuse themselves by saying of professed Christians, "I am as good as they are. They are no more self-denying, sober, or circumspect in their conduct than I am. They love pleasure and self-indulgence as well as I do." Thus they make the faults of others an excuse for their own neglect of duty. But the sins and defects of others do not excuse anyone, for the Lord has not given us an erring human pattern. The spotless Son of God has been given as our example, and those who complain of the wrong course of professed Christians are the ones who should show better lives and nobler examples. If they have so high a conception of what a Christian should be, is not their own sin so much the greater? They know what is right, and yet refuse to do it.

Beware of procrastination. Do not put off the work of forsaking your sins and seeking purity of heart through Jesus. Here is where thousands upon thousands have erred to their eternal loss. I will not here dwell upon the shortness and uncertainty of life; but there is a terrible danger—a danger not sufficiently understood—in delaying to yield to the pleading voice of God's Holy Spirit, in choosing to live in sin; for such this delay really is. Sin, however small it may be esteemed, can be indulged in only at the peril of infinite loss. What we do not overcome, will overcome us and work out our destruction.

Adam and Eve persuaded themselves that in so small a matter as eating of the forbidden fruit there could not result such terrible consequences as God had declared. But this small matter was the transgression of God's immutable and holy law, and it separated man from God and opened the floodgates of death and untold woe upon our world. Age after age there has gone up from our earth a continual cry of mourning, and the whole creation groaneth and travaileth together in pain as a consequence of man's disobedience. Heaven itself has felt the effects of his rebellion against God. Calvary stands as a memorial of the amazing sacrifice required to atone for the transgression of the divine law. Let us not regard sin as a trivial thing.

The love and suffering and death of the Son of God all testify to the terrible enormity of sin.

(9) Every act of transgression, every neglect or rejection of the grace of Christ, is reacting upon yourself; it is hardening the heart, depraving the will, benumbing the understanding, and not only making you less inclined to yield, but less capable of yielding, to the tender pleading of God's Holy Spirit.

Many are quieting a troubled conscience with the thought that they can change a course of evil when they choose; that they can trifle with the invitations of mercy, and yet be again and again impressed. They think that after doing despite to the Spirit of grace, after casting their influence on the side of Satan, in a moment of terrible extremity they can change their course. But this is not so easily done. The experience, the education, of a lifetime, has so thoroughly molded the character that few then desire to receive the image of Jesus.

Even one wrong trait of character, one sinful desire, persistently cherished, will eventually neutralize all the power of the gospel. Every sinful indulgence strengthens the soul's aversion to God. The man who manifests an infidel hardihood, or a stolid indifference to divine truth, is but reaping the harvest of that which

EFFECTS OF SIN

PLEASE, SOMEBODY LOVE ME!

Sharon was raised as a Christian, did well in school, but had few true friends. She envied other girls who had dating opportunities, and she felt unattractive and lonely. Everything she tried seemed to be ignored. Overwhelmed with rejection, Sharon lost interest in school and religion.

Craving acceptance and wanting to belong, she went on a blind date. Phil had a body like Arnold Schwarzenegger, was an all-star athlete, and drove a fiery red Porsche. As their relationship grew, so did Phil's hands. Sharon ignored her strong reservations and gave in to Phil's demands for sex. Fighting her nagging conscience, she continued dating because she felt her cycle of loneliness would repeat itself. Unfortunately, she developed a reputation for being "easy" and she became pregnant.

Loneliness is painful, but God cares. Satan tempts us harder when our eyes are not on Christ. The indicated paragraph (see 9 on page 31) will give you some idea of how important it is to accept the grace of Christ.

- How can the grace of Christ help Sharon to overcome her feelings of loneliness?
- When we are hurting, what does yielding to the Holy Spirit involve?

CONSIDER...

- writing a letter to Jesus, explaining your struggles and trials when you feel tempted.
- beginning a prayer journal with requests and answers to prayer.

FOR MORE SEE...

- Psalm 16
- Psalm 37: 3-5
- James 4:17

—CF

he has himself sown. In all the Bible there is not a more fearful warning against trifling with evil than the words of the wise man that the sinner "shall be holden with the cords of his sins." Proverbs 5:22.

Christ is ready to set us free from sin, but He does not force the will; and if by persistent transgression the will itself is wholly bent on evil, and we do not desire to be set free, if we will not accept His grace, what more can He do? We have destroyed ourselves by our determined rejection of His love. "Behold, now is the accepted time; behold, now is the day of salvation." "Today if ye will hear His voice, harden not your hearts." 2 Corinthians 6:2; Hebrews 3:7, 8.

"Man looketh on the outward appearance, but the Lord looketh on the heart"—the human heart, with its conflicting emotions of joy and sorrow; the wandering, wayward heart, which is the abode of so much impurity and deceit. 1 Samuel 16:7. He knows its motives, its very intents and purposes. Go to Him with your soul all stained as it is. Like the psalmist, throw its chambers open to the all-seeing eye, exclaiming, "Search me, O God, and know my heart: try me, and know my thoughts: and see if there be any wicked way in me, and lead me in the way everlasting." Psalm 139: 23, 24.

Many accept an intellectual religion, a form of godliness, when the heart is not cleansed. Let it be your prayer, "Create in me a clean heart, O God; and renew a right spirit within me." Psalm 51:10. Deal truly with your own soul. Be as earnest, as persistent, as you would be if your mortal life were at stake. This is a matter to be settled between God and your own soul, settled for eternity. A supposed hope, and nothing more, will prove your ruin.

Study God's word prayerfully. That word presents before you, in the law of God and the life of Christ, the great principles of holiness, without which "no man shall see the Lord." Hebrews

12:14. It convinces of sin; it plainly reveals the way of salvation. Give heed to it as the voice of God speaking to your soul.

As you see the enormity of sin, as you see yourself as you really are, do not give up to despair. It was sinners that Christ came to save. We have not to reconcile God to us, but—O wondrous love!—God in Christ is "reconciling the world unto Himself." 2 Corinthians 5:19. He is wooing by His tender love the hearts of His erring children. No earthly parent could be as patient with the faults and mistakes of his children, as is God with those He seeks to save. No one could plead more tenderly with the transgressor. No human lips ever poured out more tender entreaties to the wanderer than does He. All His promises, His warnings, are but the breathing of unutterable love.

When Satan comes to tell you that you are a great sinner, look up to your Redeemer and talk of His merits. That which will help you is to look to His light. Acknowledge your sin, but tell the enemy that "Christ Jesus came into the world to save sinners" and that you may be saved by His matchless love. 1 Timothy 1:15. Jesus asked Simon a question in regard to two debtors. One owed his lord a small sum, and the other owed him a very large sum; but he forgave them both, and Christ asked Simon which debtor would love his lord most. Simon answered, "He to whom he forgave most." Luke 7:43. We have been great sinners, but Christ died that we might be forgiven. The merits of His sacrifice are sufficient to present to the Father in our behalf. Those to whom He has forgiven most will love Him most, and will stand nearest to His throne to praise Him for His great love and infinite sacrifice. It is when we most fully comprehend the love of God that we best realize the sinfulness of sin. When we see the length of the chain that was let down for us, when we understand something of the infinite sacrifice that Christ has made in our behalf, the heart is melted with tenderness and contrition.

CONFESSION

"He that covereth his sins shall not prosper: but whoso confesseth and forsaketh them shall have mercy." Proverbs 28:13.

The conditions of obtaining mercy of God are simple and just and reasonable. The Lord does not require us to do some grievous thing in order that we may have the forgiveness of sin. We need not make long and wearisome pilgrimages, or perform painful penances, to commend our souls to the God of heaven or to expiate our transgression; but he that confesseth and forsaketh his sin shall have mercy.

The apostle says, "Confess your faults one to another, and pray one for another, that ye may be healed." James 5:16. Confess your sins to God, who only can forgive them, and your faults to one another. If you have given offense to your friend or neighbor, you are to acknowledge your wrong, and it is his duty freely to forgive you. Then you are to seek the forgiveness of God, because the brother you have wounded is the property of God, and in injuring him you sinned against his Creator and Redeemer. The case is brought before the only true Mediator, our great High Priest, who "was in all points tempted like as we are, yet without sin," and who is "touched with the feeling of our infirmities," and is able to cleanse from every stain of iniquity. Hebrews 4:15.

The Lord does not require us to do some grievous thing in order that we may have the forgiveness of sin.

Those who have not humbled their souls before God in acknowledging their guilt, have not yet fulfilled the first condition of acceptance. If we have not experienced that repentance which is not to be repented of, and have not with true humiliation of soul and brokenness of spirit confessed our sins, abhorring our iniquity, we have never truly sought for the forgiveness of sin; and if we have never sought, we have never found the peace of God. The only reason why we do not have remission of sins that are past is that we are not willing

FORGIVENESS

HOUNDING AFTER HEAVEN

A criminal escapes. Guards assemble for the hunt. Leading the way is an animal whose nose is more than *3 million times* more sensitive than a human being's: the bloodhound.

Bloodhounds aren't used for normal sport hunting. According to one trainer, taking a bloodhound rabbit hunting would be like "driving a Ferrari to the 7-Eleven–highly impractical." The bloodhound's nose is simply too focused for general sniffing. These dogs lock onto a single scent, then pursue its owner relentlessly. Unless restrained, a bloodhound will sometimes sustain the hunt to the point of exhaustion.

Some *people* are bloodhounds. One dictionary describes such an individual as "a person who pursues keenly or relentlessly."

God's forgiveness is not secured by hounding after Him. He is coming toward you, not running away. If you want to get your life back in line with His purposes, simply admit your struggle. Then give up the chase and accept His love for you. The indicated paragraph (see 10 on page 35) shows how to take the first step.

- What do you think God feels when His children ask forgiveness?
- What is there currently in your life that has you hounding after God's forgiveness?

CONSIDER...

- lighting a candle. The flame is sin. Blow out the candle. That is forgiveness.
- "talking to yourself" by writing your thoughts about forgiveness. Is there something in your background that makes forgiveness difficult to accept?

FOR MORE, SEE...

- Psalm 52
- John 8:1-11
- 1 John 1:9

—RF

to humble our hearts and comply with the conditions of the word of truth. Explicit instruction is given concerning this matter. Confession of sin, whether public or private, should be heartfelt and freely expressed. It is not to be urged from the sinner. It is not to be made in a flippant and careless way, or forced from those who have no realizing sense of the abhorrent character of sin. The confession that is the outpouring of the inmost soul finds its way to the God of infinite pity. The psalmist says, "The Lord is nigh unto them that are of a broken heart; and saveth such as be of a contrite spirit." Psalm 34:18.

True confession is always of a specific character, and acknowledges particular sins. They may be of such a nature as to be brought before God only; they may be wrongs that should be confessed to individuals who have suffered injury through them; or they may be of a public character, and should then be as publicly confessed. But all confession should be definite and to the point, acknowledging the very sins of which you are guilty.

In the days of Samuel the Israelites wandered from God. They were suffering the consequences of sin; for they had lost their faith in God, lost their discernment of His power and wisdom to rule the nation, lost their confidence in His ability to defend and vindicate His cause. They turned from the great Ruler of the universe and desired to be governed as were the nations around them. Before they found peace they made this definite confession: "We have added unto all our sins this evil, to ask us a king." 1 Samuel 12:19. The very sin of which they were convicted had to be confessed. Their ingratitude oppressed their souls and severed them from God.

(11) Confession will not be acceptable to God without sincere repentance and reformation. There must be decided changes in the life; everything offensive to God must be put away. This will be the result of genuine sorrow for sin. The work that we have to do on

our part is plainly set before us: "Wash you, make you clean; put away the evil of your doings from before Mine eyes; cease to do evil; learn to do well; seek judgment, relieve the oppressed, judge the fatherless, plead for the widow." Isaiah 1:16, 17. "If the wicked restore the pledge, give again that he had robbed, walk in the statutes of life, without committing iniquity; he shall surely live,

LIFE CHANGES

JUST DO IT!

At the 1992 French Open Tennis Tournament, 21-year-old Jim Courier won the men's singles championship for the second year in a row. Eighteen months before that he wasn't even ranked in the top 10 players in the world. But he knew he could be the number one player in the world, and he decided to do something about it.

He changed coaches and started an intense practice and exercise program. Those choices paid off. His first major win was the 1991 French Open, and he won the 1992 Australian Open as well.

Jim Courier has shown the tennis world that he can be Number One. He made the changes necessary to accomplish his goal.

What Jim Courier did to become the best male tennis player in the world is a lot like what we need to do when we choose to follow Christ. We have to make changes.

Just saying you're a Christian doesn't make it happen. Read the indicated paragraph (see 11 on page 37). It gives an idea of what we can do to show our genuine desire to follow Christ.

- According to *Steps to Christ*, why isn't confession acceptable without changes?
- What changes do you need to make to improve your relationship with God?

CONSIDER...

- making a list of changes you feel you need to make to show genuine confession.
- working on one specific change this week. Ask God to give you the strength. Ask a trusted friend or family member to pray for you.

FOR MORE, SEE...

- Psalm 51:10-13
- Ezekiel 18:30, 31
- Philippians 4:8

—JM

he shall not die." Ezekiel 33:15. Paul says, speaking of the work of repentance: "Ye sorrowed after a godly sort, what carefulness it wrought in you, yea, what clearing of yourselves, yea, what indignation, yea, what fear, yea, what vehement desire, yea, what zeal, yea, what revenge! In all things ye have approved yourselves to be clear in this matter." 2 Corinthians 7:11.

(12) When sin has deadened the moral perceptions, the wrongdoer does not discern the defects of his character nor

S I N F U L N E S S

THE BIG PURPLE MISTAKE

Matt had been driving for only a week when it happened. With driver's education and the driving test behind him, he thought he was more qualified and capable than anyone on the road. But no one was letting him drive.

His parents had recently purchased matching cars. Mom's was red; Dad's was blue. Matt waited anxiously and his big chance came. Dad reminded him to be careful. He was. He carefully flew around corners. He carefully spun his way up the last hill. He impressed himself with his driving skills. Matt returned in cool confidence, noticing that the family was gathered around. *Here's my big chance*, Matt thought. *I'll impress them with my fine cornering skills.*

Matt zipped right up behind the red car and turned sharply in beside it. Too sharply. The new purple stripes on each car taught him a lot about driving.

Stupid? Yes. Sinful? Yes, because being sinful means thinking only about yourself. Sin specializes in leading you into doing something that you later find out was very stupid. The indicated paragraph (see (12) on page 39) will give you a better idea of how sin can lead you into trouble.

- What was selfish or sinful about driving carelessly?
- What would be a good cure for self-centeredness?

CONSIDER...

- doing something around the house without being asked.
- making a list of five people for whom you can do something selfless this week.

FOR MORE, SEE...

- Proverbs 14:12
- Jeremiah 17:9
- Matthew 5:21, 22

—*JT*

realize the enormity of the evil he has committed; and unless he yields to the convicting power of the Holy Spirit he remains in partial blindness to his sin. His confessions are not sincere and in earnest. To every acknowledgment of his guilt he adds an apology in excuse of his course, declaring that if it had not been for certain circumstances he would not have done this or that for which he is reproved.

After Adam and Eve had eaten of the forbidden fruit, they were filled with a sense of shame and terror. At first their only thought was how to excuse their sin and escape the dreaded sentence of death. When the Lord inquired concerning their sin, Adam replied, laying the guilt partly upon God and partly upon his companion: "The woman whom Thou gavest to be with me, she gave me of the tree, and I did eat." The woman put the blame upon the serpent, saying, "The serpent beguiled me, and I did eat." Genesis 3:12, 13. Why did You make the serpent? Why did You suffer him to come into Eden? These were the questions implied in her excuse for her sin, thus charging God with the responsibility of their fall. The spirit of self-justification originated in the father of lies and has been exhibited by all the sons and daughters of Adam. Confessions of this order are not inspired by the divine Spirit and will not be acceptable to God. True repentance will lead a man to bear his guilt himself and acknowledge it without deception or hypocrisy. Like the poor publican, not lifting up so much as his eyes unto heaven, he will cry, "God be merciful to me a sinner," and those who do acknowledge their guilt will be justified, for Jesus will plead His blood in behalf of the repentant soul.

After Adam and Eve had eaten of the forbidden fruit, they were filled with a sense of shame and terror.

The examples in God's word of genuine repentance and humiliation reveal a spirit of confession in which there is no excuse for sin or attempt at self-justification. Paul did not seek to shield himself; he paints his sin in its darkest hue, not attempting to lessen his guilt. He says, "Many of the saints did I shut up in prison, having received authority from the chief priests; and when they were put to death, I gave my voice against them. And I punished them oft in every synagogue, and compelled them to blaspheme; and being exceedingly mad against them, I persecuted them even unto strange cities." Acts 26:10, 11. He does not hesitate to declare that "Christ Jesus came into the world to save sinners; of whom I am chief." 1 Timothy 1:15.

The humble and broken heart, subdued by genuine repentance, will appreciate something of the love of God and the cost of Calvary; and as a son confesses to a loving father, so will the truly penitent bring all his sins before God. And it is written, "If we confess our sins, He is faithful and just to forgive us our sins, and to cleanse us from all unrighteousness." 1 John 1:9.

CONSECRATION

God's promise is, "Ye shall seek Me, and find Me, when ye shall search for Me with all your heart." Jeremiah 29:13.

The whole heart must be yielded to God, or the change can never be wrought in us by which we are to be restored to His likeness. By nature we are alienated from God. The Holy Spirit describes our condition in such words as these: "Dead in trespasses and sins;" "the whole head is sick, and the whole heart faint;" "no soundness in it." We are held fast in the snare of Satan, "taken captive by him at his will." Ephesians 2:1; Isaiah 1:5, 6; 2 Timothy 2:26. God desires to heal us, to set us free. But since this requires an entire transformation, a renewing of our whole nature, we must yield ourselves wholly to Him.

The warfare against self is the greatest battle that was ever fought. The yielding of self, surrendering all to the will of God, requires a struggle; but the soul must submit to God before it can be renewed in holiness.

The government of God is not, as Satan would make it appear, founded upon a blind submission, an unreasoning control. It appeals to the intellect and the conscience. "Come now, and let us reason together" is the Creator's invitation to the beings He has made. Isaiah 1:18. God does not force the will of His creatures. He cannot accept an homage that is not willingly and intelligently given. A mere forced submission would prevent all real development of mind or character; it would make man a mere automaton. Such is not the purpose of the Creator. He desires that man, the crowning work of His creative power, shall reach the highest possible development. He sets before us the height of blessing to which He desires to bring us through His grace. He invites us to give ourselves to Him, that He may work

His will in us. It remains for us to choose whether we will be set free from the bondage of sin, to share the glorious liberty of the sons of God.

(13) In giving ourselves to God, we must necessarily give up all that would separate us from Him. Hence the Saviour says, "Whosoever he be of you that forsaketh not all that he hath, he cannot be My disciple." Luke 14:33. Whatever shall draw away the heart from God must be given up. Mammon is the idol of

I D O L S

EMPLOYEES ONLY

A cow appeared in the parking lot of a company that services airplanes. Several employees tried to herd the cow back to greener pastures, but their uniform included red shirts. The cow charged, activated an automatic door, and chased one of the employees through the lobby and into the manager's office. The employee escaped through a back door, trapped the cow in the boss's office—without an appointment—and phoned for help. For three hours the 650-pound cow demolished a coffee table, dented a desk, kicked holes in the walls, and crushed a plant. When help arrived, the uninvited guest taxied peaceably out of the office and into a waiting cow trailer.

Sometimes attempts to remove idolatry from our lives are only half-hearted. This is like wearing a red shirt and trying to shoo a cow away. Before we know it, the devil has ignored the "Employees Only" sign and is firmly entrenched in our manager's office. If we're really serious about it, the very first thing we must do is make a total commitment to remove idolatry *completely*. That's what the indicated paragraph (see (13) on page 43) is saying.

- Why is there room only for Jesus in a Christian's heart?
- What kinds of idolatry affect your life?

CONSIDER...

- looking through magazines or newspapers for examples of idolatry that threaten a Christian's life.
- reading and meditating on the words to "I Surrender All," number 309 in the *Seventh-day Adventist Hymnal*.

FOR MORE, SEE...

- Joshua 7
- Proverbs 16:3
- 1 Peter 1:13-16

—*GS*

many. The love of money, the desire for wealth, is the golden chain that binds them to Satan. Reputation and worldly honor are worshiped by another class. The life of selfish ease and freedom from responsibility is the idol of others. But these slavish bands must be broken. We cannot be half the Lord's and half the world's. We are not God's children unless we are such entirely.

There are those who profess to serve God, while they rely upon their own efforts to obey His law, to form a right character, and secure salvation. Their hearts are not moved by any deep sense of the love of Christ, but they seek to perform the duties of the Christian life as that which God requires of them in order to gain heaven. Such religion is worth nothing. When Christ dwells in the heart, the soul will be so filled with His love, with the joy of communion with Him, that it will cleave to Him; and in the contemplation of Him, self will be forgotten. Love to Christ will be the spring of action. Those who feel the constraining love of God, do not ask how little may be given to meet the requirements of God; they do not ask for the lowest standard, but aim at perfect conformity to the will of their Redeemer. With earnest desire they yield all and manifest an interest proportionate to the value of the object which they seek. A profession of Christ without this deep love is mere talk, dry formality, and heavy drudgery.

Do you feel that it is too great a sacrifice to yield all to Christ? Ask yourself the question, "What has Christ given for me?" The Son of God gave all—life and love and suffering—for our redemption. And can it be that we, the unworthy objects of so great love, will withhold our hearts from Him? Every moment of our lives we have been partakers of the blessings of His grace, and for this very reason we cannot fully realize the depths of ignorance and misery from which we have been saved. Can we look upon Him whom our sins have pierced, and yet be willing to do despite to all His love and sacrifice? In view of the infinite humiliation of the Lord of glory, shall we murmur because we can enter into life only through conflict and self-abasement?

The inquiry of many a proud heart is, "Why need I go in penitence and humiliation before I can have the assurance of my acceptance with God?" I point you to Christ. He was sinless, and, more than this, He was the Prince of heaven; but in man's behalf

SOMETHING BETTER

THE PLOT THAT BACKFIRED

At the beginning of the sixteenth century, Michelangelo was the number one artist in Italy and under contract to Pope Julius to sculpt the pope's tomb. When the massive structure was only partially completed, two rival artists, Bramante and Raphael, persuaded the pope that it would be bad luck to have his tomb finished while he was still alive. They suggested Michelangelo be assigned to paint the ceiling of a chapel the pope had built. Since Michelangelo had no experience in this type of painting, they hoped his reputation would suffer.

After much protest, Michelangelo began painting. Five years later the Sistine Chapel ceiling was completed, and his status as the greatest living artist was secure.

Although we may think we know what we want to do in life, God may have an even better plan in store for us. Read the indicated paragraph (see 14 on page 46) to discover the trade-off God has in mind.

- How is God's plan for your life different from Bramante and Raphael's plot for Michelangelo?
- What are the rewards of following God's wishes?

CONSIDER...

- looking back at the times in your life when you had to make unexpected changes in your plans. How often did those changes turn out for the best?
- interviewing a person in your church who feels God has led in his or her life. Ask how life was different before and after he or she began a relationship with God.

FOR MORE, SEE...

- Job 42:10
- Philippians 2:5-11
- Hebrews 12:5, 6
- 1 Peter 5:6, 7

—SN

He became sin for the race. "He was numbered with the transgressors; and He bare the sin of many, and made intercession for the transgressors." Isaiah 53:12.

(14) But what do we give up, when we give all? A sin-polluted heart, for Jesus to purify, to cleanse by His own blood, and to save by His matchless love. And yet men think it hard to give up all! I am ashamed to hear it spoken of, ashamed to write it.

God does not require us to give up anything that it is for our best interest to retain. In all that He does, He has the well-being of His children in view. Would that all who have not chosen Christ might realize that He has something vastly better to offer them than they are seeking for themselves. Man is doing the greatest injury and injustice to his own soul when he thinks and acts contrary to the will of God. No real joy can be found in the path forbidden by Him who knows what is best and who plans for the good of His creatures. The path of transgression is the path of misery and destruction.

It is a mistake to entertain the thought that God is pleased to see His children suffer. All heaven is interested in the happiness of man. Our heavenly Father does not close the avenues of joy to any of His creatures. The divine requirements call upon us to shun those indulgences that would bring suffering and disappointment, that would close to us the door of happiness and heaven. The world's Redeemer accepts men as they are, with all their wants, imperfections, and weaknesses; and He will not only cleanse from sin and grant redemption through His blood, but will satisfy the heart-longing of all who consent to wear His yoke, to bear His burden. It is His purpose to impart peace and rest to all who come to Him for the bread of life. He requires us to perform only those duties that will lead our steps to heights of bliss to which the disobedient can never attain. The true, joyous life of the soul is to have Christ formed within, the hope of glory.

(15) Many are inquiring, "How am I to make the surrender of myself to God?" You desire to give yourself to Him, but you are weak in moral power, in slavery to doubt, and controlled by the habits of your life of sin. Your promises and resolutions are like ropes of sand. You cannot control your thoughts, your impulses, your affections. The knowledge of your broken promises and

CHOICE

THE FIRST STEP

Myles Horton grew up among the poverty-stricken mountain people of Appalachia. "Nothing will change," Horton said to himself, "until we change." He believed that poor working-class people could take charge of their lives and circumstances. But how?

Horton studied social justice issues and visited Denmark's folk schools that tried to help the common people. But all his desire for a school stayed just that—hope—until Christmas night, 1931. Horton wrote a note to himself. "What you must do is go back, get a simple place, move in and you are there. You start with this and let it grow."

As he described it later, "A five-year burden had rolled away and I went to sleep wondering why it had taken so long. It all seemed so clear and simple—the way to get started was to start." And so Highlander School was born.

There is power in the process of making a decision and acting on it. We have to do more than just want to give ourselves to God. We have to do it, asking Him to take charge. The indicated paragraph (see (15) on page 47) will show you how to do this.

- What is similar between Myles Horton's problem and what we need to do to surrender ourselves to God?
- What choices are you making today that will affect the rest of your life?

CONSIDER...

- drawing an illustration of someone who seems to be paralyzed by indecision.
- doing something for someone else that you've never done before.

FOR MORE, SEE...

- Joshua 24:15
- Psalm 51:10
- Matthew 14:22-31

—CH

forfeited pledges weakens your confidence in your own sincerity, and causes you to feel that God cannot accept you; but you need not despair. What you need to understand is the true force of the will. This is the governing power in the nature of man, the power of decision, or of choice. Everything depends on the right action of the will. The power of choice God has given to men; it is theirs to exercise. You cannot change your heart, you cannot of yourself give to God its affections; but you can choose to serve Him. You can give Him your will; He will then work in you to will and to do according to His good pleasure. Thus your whole nature will be brought under the control of the Spirit of Christ; your affections will be centered upon Him, your thoughts will be in harmony with Him.

Through the right exercise of the will, an entire change may be made in your life.

Desires for goodness and holiness are right as far as they go; but if you stop here, they will avail nothing. Many will be lost while hoping and desiring to be Christians. They do not come to the point of yielding the will to God. They do not now *choose* to be Christians.

Through the right exercise of the will, an entire change may be made in your life. By yielding up your will to Christ, you ally yourself with the power that is above all principalities and powers. You will have strength from above to hold you steadfast, and thus through constant surrender to God you will be enabled to live the new life, even the life of faith.

FAITH AND ACCEPTANCE

As your conscience has been quickened by the Holy Spirit, you have seen something of the evil of sin, of its power, its guilt, its woe; and you look upon it with abhorrence. You feel that sin has separated you from God, that you are in bondage to the power of evil. The more you struggle to escape, the more you realize your helplessness. Your motives are impure; your heart is unclean. You see that your life has been filled with selfishness and sin. You long to be forgiven, to be cleansed, to be set free. Harmony with God, likeness to Him—what can you do to obtain it?

[16] It is peace that you need—Heaven's forgiveness and peace and love in the soul. Money cannot buy it, intellect cannot procure it, wisdom cannot attain to it; you can never hope, by your own efforts, to secure it. But God offers it to you as a gift, "without money and without price." Isaiah 55:1. It is yours if you will but reach out your hand and grasp it. The Lord says, "Though your sins be as scarlet, they shall be as white as snow; though they be red like crimson, they shall be as wool." Isaiah 1:18. "A new heart also will I give you, and a new spirit will I put within you." Ezekiel 36:26.

You have confessed your sins, and in heart put them away. You have resolved to give yourself to God. Now go to Him, and ask that He will wash away your sins and give you a new heart. Then believe that He does this *because He has promised*. This is the lesson which Jesus taught while He was on earth, that the gift which God promises us, we must believe we do receive, and it is ours. Jesus healed the people of their diseases when they had faith in His power; He helped them in the things which they could see, thus inspiring them with confidence in Him concerning things which they could not see—leading them to believe in His power to forgive sins. This He plainly stated in the healing of the man sick with palsy: "*That ye may know that the Son of man hath power on earth to forgive sins,* (then saith He to the sick of the palsy,) Arise, take up thy bed, and go unto thine house." Matthew 9:6. So also John the evangelist says, speaking of the miracles of Christ, "These are written, that ye might believe that Jesus is the

F O R G I V E N E S S

BUMPER-TO-BUMPER FORGIVENESS

Jim braked his blue Plymouth Horizon to a stop behind a brand-new red BMW at the traffic light and looked down at his list of things to do. Suddenly, he felt the car jolt, and looked up to see what was the matter. The BMW had rolled back against the front end of his car!

Just as Jim was ready to yell at the driver, he realized that the BMW driver hadn't done anything at all—it was all Jim's fault. He had unconsciously taken his foot off the brake and had rolled into the back of the BMW.

Jim expected the BMW driver to get out, check his car, and tell him off—but seconds passed, the light turned green, and the BMW drove away. Jim breathed a sigh of relief and learned a new meaning of forgiveness—and it felt good!

Forgiveness is described in the indicated paragraph (see 16 on page 49) as a gift of God. Read and find out how you can have peace of mind.

- If you were the guilty driver above, how would you find forgiveness if the BMW driver wasn't the forgiving type?
- What do you feel like when you've been forgiven? What makes you comfortable enough to forgive others?

CONSIDER...

- making a sign for your door that says, "Forgive Somebody Today."
- writing a letter to someone you've been holding a grudge against. Tell him or her that you want to be friends again.

FOR MORE, SEE...

- Matthew 18:23-35
- Luke 5:18-25
- 1 John 1:9

—KP

Christ, the Son of God; and that believing ye might have life through His name." John 20:31.

From the simple Bible account of how Jesus healed the sick, we may learn something about how to believe in Him for the forgiveness of sins. Let us turn to the story of the paralytic at Bethesda. The poor sufferer was helpless; he had not used his limbs for thirty-eight years. Yet Jesus bade him, "Rise, take up thy bed, and walk." The sick man might have said, "Lord, if Thou wilt make me whole, I will obey Thy word." But, no, he believed Christ's word, believed that he was made whole, and he made the effort at once; he *willed* to walk, and he did walk. He acted on the word of Christ, and God gave the power. He was made whole.

You cannot atone for your past sins; you cannot change your heart and make yourself holy.

In like manner you are a sinner. You cannot atone for your past sins; you cannot change your heart and make yourself holy. But God promises to do all this for you through Christ. You *believe* that promise. You confess your sins and give yourself to God. You *will* to serve Him. Just as surely as you do this, God will fulfill His word to you. If you believe the promise,—believe that you are forgiven and cleansed,—God supplies the fact; you are made whole, just as Christ gave the paralytic power to walk when the man believed that he was healed. It *is* so if you believe it.

Do not wait to *feel* that you are made whole, but say, "I believe it; it *is* so, not because I feel it, but because God has promised."

Jesus says, "What things soever ye desire, when ye pray, believe that ye receive them, and ye shall have them." Mark 11:24. There is a condition to this promise—that we pray according to the will of God. But it is the will of God to cleanse us from sin, to make us His children, and to enable us to live a holy life. So we may ask for these blessings, and believe that we receive them, and thank God that we *have* received them. It is our privilege to go to Jesus and be cleansed, and to stand before the law without shame or remorse. "There is therefore now no condemnation to them which are in Christ Jesus, who walk not after the flesh, but after the Spirit." Romans 8:1.

Some seem to feel that they must be on probation, and must prove to the Lord that they are re-formed, before they can claim His blessing.

Henceforth you are not your own; you are bought with a price. "Ye were not redeemed with corruptible things, as silver and gold; . . . but with the precious blood of Christ, as of a lamb without blemish and without spot." 1 Peter 1:18, 19. Through this simple act of believing God, the Holy Spirit has begotten a new life in your heart. You are as a child born into the family of God, and He loves you as He loves His Son.

Now that you have given yourself to Jesus, do not draw back, do not take yourself away from Him, but day by day say, "I am Christ's; I have given myself to Him;" and ask Him to give you His Spirit and keep you by His grace. As it is by giving yourself to God, and believing Him, that you become His child, so you are to live in Him. The apostle says, "As ye have therefore received Christ Jesus the Lord, so walk ye in Him." Colossians 2:6.

Some seem to feel that they must be on probation, and must prove to the Lord that they are reformed, before they can claim His blessing. But they may claim the blessing of God even now. They must have His grace, the Spirit of Christ, to help their infirmities, or they cannot resist evil. Jesus loves to have us come to Him just as we are, sinful, helpless, dependent. We may come with all our weakness, our folly, our sinfulness, and fall at His feet in penitence. It is His glory to encircle us in the arms of His love and to bind up our wounds, to cleanse us from all impurity.

(17) Here is where thousands fail; they do not believe that Jesus pardons them personally, individually. They do not take God at His word. It is the privilege of all who comply with the conditions to know for themselves that pardon is freely extended for every sin. Put away the suspicion that God's promises are not

D O U B T

NOTHING FOR ME?

"Hey, what about, Dorothy?" the scarecrow asked the Wizard of Oz after the wizard had given the scarecrow a diploma, the lion a medal, and the tin man a heart-shaped watch.

"Oh, I don't think there's anything in that black bag for me," said Dorothy before the wizard could answer.

Dorothy was right in one sense. There was nothing *in the bag* for her. But what she wanted most—to go home—had already been promised to her. She just needed to believe that it was possible. Dorothy had a reason not to believe. The wizard had deceived her once. We, on the other hand, have every reason to believe. God is not an imaginary wizard. He is real, He does not lie, and He has a promise with your name on it. The indicated paragraph (see (17) on page 53) will tell you more.

- Do you sometimes feel like Dorothy—that what has been promised in the Bible is not for you? Why do you think so?
- What does it mean to receive God's promises?

CONSIDER...

- praying that God will help you to learn how to claim His promises for your very own.
- every day for a week, claiming one promise you have difficulty accepting.

FOR MORE, SEE...

- Isaiah 49:15, 16
- Mark 9:14-29
- Mark 11:24

—VF

meant for you. They are for every repentant transgressor. Strength and grace have been provided through Christ to be brought by ministering angels to every believing soul. None are so sinful that they cannot find strength, purity, and righteousness in Jesus, who died for them. He is waiting to strip them of their garments stained and polluted with sin, and to put upon them the white robes of righteousness; He bids them live and not die.

God does not deal with us as finite men deal with one another. His thoughts are thoughts of mercy, love, and tenderest compassion. He says, "Let the wicked forsake his way, and the unrighteous man his thoughts: and let him return unto the Lord, and He will have mercy upon him; and to our God, for He will abundantly pardon." "I have blotted out, as a thick cloud, thy transgressions, and, as a cloud, thy sins." Isaiah 55:7; 44:22.

"I have no pleasure in the death of him that dieth, saith the Lord God: wherefore turn yourselves, and live ye." Ezekiel 18:32. Satan is ready to steal away the blessed assurances of God. He desires to take every glimmer of hope and every ray of light from the soul; but you must not permit him to do this. Do not give ear to the tempter, but say, "Jesus has died that I might live. He loves me, and wills not that I should perish. I have a compassionate heavenly Father; and although I have abused His love, though the blessings He has given me have been squandered, I will arise, and go to my Father, and say, 'I have sinned against heaven, and before Thee, and am no more worthy to be called Thy son: make me as one of Thy hired servants.'" The parable tells you how the wanderer will be received: "*When he was yet a great way off,* his father saw him, and had compassion, and ran, and fell on his neck, and kissed him." Luke 15:18-20.

But even this parable, tender and touching as it is, comes short of expressing the infinite compassion of the heavenly Father. The Lord declares by His prophet, "I have loved thee with an everlasting love: *therefore with loving-kindness have I drawn thee."* Jeremiah 31:3. While the sinner is yet far from the Father's house, wasting his substance in a strange country, the Father's heart is yearning over him; and every longing awakened in the soul to return to God is but the tender pleading of His Spirit, wooing, entreating, drawing the wanderer to his Father's heart of love.

(18) With the rich promises of the Bible before you, can you give place to doubt? Can you believe that when the poor sinner

G O D ' S L O V E

DEADLY QUESTION

Cambyses, the son of Cyrus the Great, was not an easy king to please. He liked to ask people what they thought of him. But if the answer didn't quite suit him, it could well mean death.

The Greek historian Herodotus, however, reported in the fifth century B.C., that at least one courtier came up with a winning answer to the fateful question. In fact, it has to be one of the most diplomatic answers in history: "I do not think you are equal to your father, for you do not yet have a son like the son he left behind him in yourself."

Cambyses mulled that answer over for a while and decided to spare the man's life—probably because he wasn't sure what to think. But it must have been a very worrisome thing to be working for Cambyses, wondering what to say if he asked the deadly question.

Fortunately we have a King who doesn't ask dangerous questions. He isn't moody or unpredictable. Whatever He does for you is done "always in love." Read the indicated paragraph (see (18) on page 55) to discover how you never need to doubt Jesus' love for you.

- In what ways are Jesus and Cambyses different?
- How should Jesus' love for us affect how we treat others?

CONSIDER...

- asking God to help you develop a Christlike love for those around you.
- contrasting Jesus' love with that expressed in a currently popular love song.

FOR MORE, SEE...

- Psalm 103:6-14
- John 3:16
- Ephesians 2:4-7

—*GS*

longs to return, longs to forsake his sins, the Lord sternly withholds him from coming to His feet in repentance? Away with such thoughts! Nothing can hurt your own soul more than to entertain such a conception of our heavenly Father. He hates sin, but He loves the sinner, and He gave Himself in the person of Christ, that all who would might be saved and have eternal blessedness in the kingdom of glory. What stronger or more tender language could have been employed than He has chosen in which to express His love toward us? He declares, "Can a woman forget her sucking child, that she should not have compassion on the son of her womb? yea, they may forget, yet will I not forget thee." Isaiah 49:15.

Look up, you that are doubting and trembling; for Jesus lives to make intercession for us. Thank God for the gift of His dear Son and pray that He may not have died for you in vain. The Spirit invites you today. Come with your whole heart to Jesus, and you may claim His blessing.

The great heart of Infinite Love is drawn toward the sinner with boundless compassion.

As you read the promises, remember they are the expression of unutterable love and pity. The great heart of Infinite Love is drawn toward the sinner with boundless compassion. "We have redemption through His blood, the forgiveness of sins." Ephesians 1:7. Yes, only believe that God is your helper. He wants to restore His moral image in man. As you draw near to Him with confession and repentance, He will draw near to you with mercy and forgiveness.

THE TEST OF DISCIPLESHIP

"If any man be in Christ, he is a new creature: old things are passed away; behold, all things are become new." 2 Corinthians 5:17.

[19] A person may not be able to tell the exact time or place, or trace all the chain of circumstances in the process of conversion; but this does not prove him to be unconverted. Christ said to Nicodemus, "The wind bloweth where it listeth, and thou hearest the sound thereof, but canst not tell whence it cometh, and whither it goeth: so is everyone that is born of the Spirit." John 3:8. Like the wind, which is invisible, yet the effects of which are plainly seen and felt, is the Spirit of God in its work upon the human heart. That regenerating power, which no human eye can see, begets a new life in the soul; it creates a new being in the image of God. While the work of the Spirit is silent and imperceptible, its effects are manifest. If the heart has been renewed by the Spirit of God, the life will bear witness to the fact. While we cannot do anything to change our hearts or to bring ourselves into harmony with God; while we must not trust at all to ourselves or our good works, our lives will reveal whether the grace of God is dwelling within us. A change will be seen in the character, the habits, the pursuits. The contrast will be clear and decided between what they have been and what they are. The character is revealed, not by occasional good deeds and occasional misdeeds, but by the tendency of the habitual words and acts.

It is true that there may be an outward correctness of deportment without the renewing power of Christ. The love of influence and the desire for the esteem of others may produce a well-ordered life. Self-respect may lead us to avoid the appearance of evil. A selfish heart may perform generous actions. By what means, then, shall we determine whose side we are on?

Who has the heart? With whom are our thoughts? Of whom do we love to converse? Who has our warmest affections and our best energies? If we are Christ's, our thoughts are with Him, and our sweetest thoughts are of Him. All we have and are is

RE-CREATION

DREAM GIFT

One day Sheila and Dan received an invitation from an attorney's office to attend a special dinner at a nearby hotel. A white limousine pulled into the driveway on the designated day to pick them up.

They were greeted by a "Fred McGillicudy," who reported that Dan's distant uncle had passed away. In his will the uncle had left just two round-trip tickets to Hawaii and some beach paraphernalia. Unfortunately, Dan and Sheila were left with just the beach gear. Fred presented them with beach towels, suntan lotion—even a beach ball on a silver platter.

The limousine ride home was uneventful until the driver jerked over to the side of the road and someone jumped in the car. He presented them with two all-expense-paid tickets to Hawaii. To this day Dan and Sheila have no idea who was behind this dream gift.

But you have the joy of knowing Who gives you the gift of life. Even though you can't see Jesus face to face as He works in your life, you can know He's there. Read the indicated paragraph (see 19 on page 57) to learn more about the quiet way Christ re-creates you!

- Why do you think Jesus works without fanfare in your life?
- How do you feel knowing Jesus keeps His work in you just between you and Him?

CONSIDER...

- listing three ways Jesus has helped you change for the better.
- sending a small gift to someone in need—anonymously.

FOR MORE, SEE...

- Ezekiel 11:19
- Acts 9:1-18
- Titus 3:3-7

—*LC*

consecrated to Him. We long to bear His image, breathe His spirit, do His will, and please Him in all things.

Those who become new creatures in Christ Jesus will bring forth the fruits of the Spirit, "love, joy, peace, long-suffering, gentleness, goodness, faith, meekness, temperance." Galatians 5:22, 23. They will no longer fashion themselves according to the former lusts, but by the faith of the Son of God they will follow in His steps, reflect His character, and purify themselves even as He is pure. The things they once hated they now love, and the things they once loved they hate. The proud and self-assertive become meek and lowly in heart. The vain and supercilious become serious and unobtrusive. The drunken become sober, and the profligate pure. The vain customs and fashions of the world are laid aside. Christians will seek not the "outward adorning," but "the hidden man of the heart, in that which is not corruptible, even the ornament of a meek and quiet spirit." 1 Peter 3:3, 4.

There is no evidence of genuine repentance unless it works reformation.

There is no evidence of genuine repentance unless it works reformation. If he restore the pledge, give again that he had robbed, confess his sins, and love God and his fellow men, the sinner may be sure that he has passed from death unto life.

When, as erring, sinful beings, we come to Christ and become partakers of His pardoning grace, love springs up in the heart. Every burden is light, for the yoke that Christ imposes is easy. Duty becomes a delight, and sacrifice a pleasure. The path that before seemed shrouded in darkness, becomes bright with beams from the Sun of Righteousness.

The loveliness of the character of Christ will be seen in His followers. It was His delight to do the will of God. Love to God, zeal for His glory, was the controlling power in our Saviour's life. Love beautified and ennobled all His actions. Love is of God. The unconsecrated heart cannot originate or produce it. It is found only in the heart where Jesus reigns. "We love, because He first loved us." 1 John 4:19, R.V. In the heart renewed by divine grace, love is the principle of action. It modifies the character, governs the impulses, controls the passions, subdues enmity, and ennobles the affections. This love, cherished in the soul, sweetens the life and sheds a refining influence on all around.

Obedience is not a mere outward compliance, but the service of love.

There are two errors against which the children of God—particularly those who have just come to trust in His grace—especially need to guard. The first, already dwelt upon, is that of looking to their own works, trusting to anything they can do, to bring themselves into harmony with God. He who is trying to become holy by his own works in keeping the law, is attempting an impossibility. All that man can do without Christ is polluted with selfishness and sin. It is the grace of Christ alone, through faith, that can make us holy.

The opposite and no less dangerous error is that belief in Christ releases men from keeping the law of God; that since by faith alone we become partakers of the grace of Christ, our works have nothing to do with our redemption.

(20) But notice here that obedience is not a mere outward compliance, but the service of love. The law of God is an expression of His very nature; it is an embodiment of the great principle of love, and hence is the foundation of His government

in heaven and earth. If our hearts are renewed in the likeness of God, if the divine love is implanted in the soul, will not the law of God be carried out in the life? When the principle of love is implanted in the heart, when man is renewed after the image of Him that created him, the new-covenant promise is fulfilled, "I will put My laws into their hearts, and in their minds will I write them." Hebrews 10:16. And if the law is written in the heart, will it not

O B E D I E N C E

TREVOR'S BLANKET STATEMENT

Eleven-year-old Trevor Ferrell saw a television report on Philadelphia's inner-city homeless. He couldn't believe people actually lived on the streets. With his parents' help, he collected as many blankets as he could and they drove downtown.

A block past city hall, they spotted an emaciated figure huddled on a sidewalk grate. Trevor got out of the car and approached the man.

"Sir," he said, "here's a blanket for you."

The man stared up at Trevor. "Thank you," he said softly. "God bless you."

Trevor later found himself explaining what he was doing to reporters: "It's Jesus in me that makes me want to do this."

Trevor discovered that service is the secret of obedience to God's commandments. You may be trying to obey God without His love in your heart. The paragraph indicated (see 20 on page 60) will give you insights into what obedience is all about.

- How long do you think Trevor's help to the homeless would have lasted if it were not based on love?
- What is the difference between obeying God because you love Him and obeying Him because your parents tell you to do so?

CONSIDER...

- reading hymn number 590 in the *Seventh-day Adventist Hymnal*. Write a short paragraph about what you think the author intended to say in the hymn.
- contacting a voluntary organization in our community to see how you can get involved in its work.

FOR MORE, SEE...

- 1 Samuel 15:22
- Psalm 119:33-35
- Romans 5:19

—ST

shape the life? Obedience—the service and allegiance of love—is the true sign of discipleship. Thus the Scripture says, "This is the love of God, that we keep His commandments." "He that saith, I know Him, and keepeth not His commandments, is a liar, and the truth is not in him." 1 John 5:3, 2:4. Instead of releasing man from obedience, it is faith, and faith only, that makes us partakers of the grace of Christ, which enables us to render obedience.

We do not earn salvation by our obedience; for salvation is the free gift of God, to be received by faith. But obedience is the fruit of faith. "Ye know that He was manifested to take away our sins; and in Him is no sin. Whosoever abideth in Him sinneth not: whosoever sinneth hath not seen Him, neither known Him." 1 John 3:5, 6. Here is the true test. If we abide in Christ, if the love of God dwells in us, our feelings, our thoughts, our purposes, our actions, will be in harmony with the will of God as expressed in the precepts of His holy law. "Little children, let no man deceive you: he that doeth righteousness is righteous, even as He is righteous." 1 John 3:7. Righteousness is defined by the standard of God's holy law, as expressed in the ten precepts given on Sinai.

We do not earn salvation by our obedience; for salvation is the free gift of God, to be received by faith.

That so-called faith in Christ which professes to release men from the obligation of obedience to God, is not faith, but presumption. "By grace are ye saved through faith." But "faith, if it hath not works, is dead." Ephesians 2:8, James 2:17. Jesus said of Himself before He came to earth, "I delight to do Thy will, O My God: yea, Thy law is within My heart." Psalm 40:8. And just before He ascended again to heaven He declared, "I have kept My Father's commandments, and abide in His love." John 15:10.

The Scripture says, "Hereby we do know that we know Him, if we keep His commandments. . . . He that saith he abideth in Him ought himself also so to walk even as He walked." 1 John 2:3-6. "Because Christ also suffered for us, leaving us an example, that ye should follow His steps." 1 Peter 2:21.

The condition of eternal life is now just what it always has been,—just what it was in Paradise before the fall of our first parents,—perfect obedience to the law of God, perfect righteousness. If eternal life were granted on any condition short of this, then the happiness of the whole universe would be imperiled. The way would be open for sin, with all its train of woe and misery, to be immortalized.

It was possible for Adam, before the fall, to form a righteous character by obedience to God's law. But he failed to do this, and because of his sin our natures are fallen and we cannot make ourselves righteous. Since we are sinful, unholy, we cannot perfectly obey the holy law. We have no righteousness of our own with which to meet the claims of the law of God. But Christ has made a way of escape for us. He lived on earth amid trials and temptations such as we have to meet. He lived a sinless life. He died for us, and now He offers to take our sins and give us His righteousness. If you give yourself to Him, and accept Him as your Saviour, then, sinful as your life may have been, for His sake you are accounted righteous. Christ's character stands in place of your character, and you are accepted before God just as if you had not sinned.

More than this, Christ changes the heart. He abides in your heart by faith. You are to maintain this connection with Christ by faith and the continual surrender of your will to Him; and so long as you do this, He will work in you to will and to do according to His good pleasure. So you may say, "The life which I now live in the flesh I live by the faith of the Son of God, who loved me, and gave Himself for me." Galatians 2:20. So Jesus said to His disciples, "It is not ye that speak, but the Spirit of your Father which speaketh in you." Matthew 10:20. Then with Christ working in you, you will manifest the same spirit and do the same good works—works of righteousness, obedience.

So we have nothing in ourselves of which to boast. We have no ground for self-exaltation. Our only ground of hope is in the

P E R F E C T I O N

TRYING TO GET IT RIGHT

Everyone knows that Thomas Edison invented the electric light. What many people don't realize is that he failed thousands of times before he finally come up with a light that actually worked. If he had gotten discouraged every time he failed, he never would have invented anything.

"When I want to discover something, I begin by reading up on everything that has been done along that line in the past," he once said. "I gather the data of many thousands of experiments as a starting point, and then I make thousands more."

Edison and his staff also failed thousands of times in trying to invent a working electric battery. When a friend of Edison's tried to console him, Edison replied, "Why, man, I've got a lot of results. I now know several thousand things that won't work!"

Sometimes it seems that no matter how many times you try, you still don't get it right. Fortunately God doesn't expect you to be perfect. Read the indicated paragraph (see 21 on page 63) to see how you can succeed—even when you fail.

- Why is it impossible for humans to be perfect?
- What would your life be like if you had to be perfect all the time?

CONSIDER...

- talking to an adult you admire who seems to have a perfect life. Ask how he or she does it.
- reading an article about how top athletes train for their sports. Do they ever reach "perfection"?

FOR MORE, SEE...

- Romans 1:17
- Romans 5:6-8
- Ephesians 4:17-24

—CD

righteousness of Christ imputed to us, and in that wrought by His Spirit working in and through us. When we speak of faith, there is a distinction that should be borne in mind. There is a kind of belief that is wholly distinct from faith. The existence and power of God, the truth of His word, are facts that even Satan and his hosts cannot at heart deny. The Bible says that "the devils also believe, and tremble;" but this is not faith. James 2:19. Where there is not only a belief in God's word, but a submission of the will to Him; where the heart is yielded to Him, the affections fixed upon Him, there is faith—faith that works by love and purifies the soul. Through this faith the heart is renewed in the image of God. And the heart that in its unrenewed state is not subject to the law of God, neither indeed can be, now delights in its holy precepts, exclaiming with the psalmist, "O how love I Thy law! it is my meditation all the day." Psalm 119:97. And the righteousness of the law is fulfilled in us, "who walk not after the flesh, but after the Spirit." Romans 8:1.

We have nothing in ourselves of which to boast.

There are those who have known the pardoning love of Christ and who really desire to be children of God, yet they realize that their character is imperfect, their life faulty, and they are ready to doubt whether their hearts have been renewed by the Holy Spirit. To such I would say, Do not draw back in despair. We shall often have to bow down and weep at the feet of Jesus because of our shortcomings and mistakes, but we are not to be discouraged. Even if we are overcome by the enemy, we are not cast off, not forsaken and rejected of God. No; Christ is at the right hand of God, who also maketh intercession for us. Said the beloved John, "These things write I unto you, that ye sin not. And if any man sin, we have an advocate with the Father, Jesus Christ the righteous." 1 John 2:1. And do not forget the words of Christ, "The Father Himself loveth you." John 16:27. He desires to restore you to Himself, to see His own purity and holiness reflected in you. And if you will but yield yourself to Him, He that hath begun a good work in you will carry it forward to the day of Jesus Christ. Pray more fervently; believe more fully. As we come to distrust our own power, let us trust the power of our Redeemer, and we shall praise Him who is the health of our countenance.

S E L F - V I S I O N

I'M NOT GOOD ENOUGH

Ten-year-old Wesley loved and admired his 20-year-old brother, Todd—so much so that he tried to copy Todd in almost every way. Wesley combed his hair like Todd and walked and talked like him too. He felt better about himself when he acted like Todd. Sometimes Wesley would get discouraged because he didn't feel good enough in many ways. He couldn't shoot a basketball as well as Todd, he couldn't play the piano, he couldn't drive a car or have a bunch of cool friends to hang out with. Not yet anyway.

When Todd took time with Wesley, it made Wes feel happy, and gave him the desire to be with Todd even more so he could one day be just like him.

You have a big brother. His name is Jesus. He wants to be with you all the time. He doesn't just tolerate you, He loves you! You don't need to feel discouraged about not being good enough. He'll be happy to help you; just ask Him. The indicated paragraph (see 22 on page 67) will tell you more.

- What do you see in Wesley that is most like yourself? In Todd?
- When you compare yourself to Jesus, how should it make you feel?

CONSIDER...

- joining a Big Brother or Big Sister association in your town.
- making a list of things about yourself that you could improve with practice and God's help.

FOR MORE, SEE...

- Psalm 147
- Luke 15:11-32
- Romans 12

—KB

(22) The closer you come to Jesus, the more faulty you will appear in your own eyes; for your vision will be clearer, and your imperfections will be seen in broad and distinct contrast to His perfect nature. This is evidence that Satan's delusions have lost their power; that the vivifying influence of the Spirit of God is arousing you.

The closer you come to Jesus, the more faulty you will appear in your own eyes.

No deep-seated love for Jesus can dwell in the heart that does not realize its own sinfulness. The soul that is transformed by the grace of Christ will admire His divine character; but if we do not see our own moral deformity, it is unmistakable evidence that we have not had a view of the beauty and excellence of Christ.

The less we see to esteem in ourselves, the more we shall see to esteem in the infinite purity and loveliness of our Saviour. A view of our sinfulness drives us to Him who can pardon; and when the soul, realizing its helplessness, reaches out after Christ, He will reveal Himself in power. The more our sense of need drives us to Him and to the word of God, the more exalted views we shall have of His character, and the more fully we shall reflect His image.

GROWING UP INTO CHRIST

The change of heart by which we become children of God is in the Bible spoken of as birth. Again, it is compared to the germination of the good seed sown by the husbandman. In like manner those who are just converted to Christ are, "as newborn babes," to "grow up" to the stature of men and women in Christ Jesus. 1 Peter 2:2; Ephesians 4:15. Or like the good seed sown in the field, they are to grow up and bring forth fruit. Isaiah says that they shall "be called trees of righteousness, the planting of the Lord, that He might be glorified." Isaiah 61:3. So from natural life, illustrations are drawn, to help us better to understand the mysterious truths of spiritual life.

(23) Not all the wisdom and skill of man can produce life in the smallest object in nature. It is only through the life which God Himself has imparted, that either plant or animal can live. So it is only through the life from God that spiritual life is begotten in the hearts of men. Unless a man is "born from above," he cannot become a partaker of the life which Christ came to give. John 3:3, margin. As with life, so it is with growth. It is God who brings the bud to bloom and the flower to fruit. It is by His power that the seed develops, "first the blade, then the ear, after that the full corn in the ear." Mark 4:28. And the prophet Hosea says of Israel, that "he shall grow as the lily." "They shall revive as the corn, and grow as the vine." Hosea 14:5, 7. And Jesus bids us "consider the lilies how they grow." Luke 12:27. The plants and flowers grow not by their own care or anxiety or effort, but by receiving that which God has furnished to minister to their life. The child cannot, by any anxiety or power of its own, add to its

stature. No more can you, by anxiety or effort of yourself, secure spiritual growth. The plant, the child, grows by receiving from its surroundings that which ministers to its life—air, sunshine, and food. What these gifts of nature are to animal and plant, such is Christ to those who trust in Him. He is their "everlasting light," "a sun and shield." Isaiah 60:19; Psalm 84:11. He shall be as "the dew unto Israel." "He shall come down like rain upon the mown

MIRACLE OF LIFE

BURIED ALIVE

The Michigan Bulb Company catalog made Teresa feel as though she could be a prize-winning gardener. Tulips, lilies, irises, and roses decorated the shiny pages. She spent hours deciding what she wanted and finally ordered 75 tulips and irises.

Teresa could hardly wait for those bulbs to arrive. When the brown packages were finally delivered, however, she was disappointed. The bulbs looked positively dead.

Determined to have her flower garden, she carefully followed directions and planted the bulbs. Then winter snows blanketed the yard. It was easy to forget that the bulbs were out there.

One spring day she noticed several green shoots pushing up through the earth. There they were! All 75 of those bulbs made it through the winter. Teresa knew only God could have given them life. It surely wasn't anything that she had done.

God can do that with your spiritual life also. Read the indicated paragraph (see 23 on page 68). God is the only one who can give physical *and* spiritual life.

- Why is it important to know who the Life-giver is?
- What examples of God's creation and re-creation have impressed you personally?

CONSIDER...

- thinking about someone you know who's received the gift of spiritual life. Make a list of ways they are different.
- planting a seed. As you watch for signs of new life, think about the One who gives life and about what you did to produce life.

FOR MORE, SEE...

- Genesis 2:7
- John 3:1-8
- 2 Corinthians 5:17

—JM

grass." Hosea 14:5; Psalm 72:6. He is the living water, "the Bread of God . . . which cometh down from heaven, and giveth life unto the world." John 6:33.

In the matchless gift of His Son, God has encircled the whole world with an atmosphere of grace as real as the air which circulates around the globe. All who choose to breathe this life-giving atmosphere will live and grow up to the stature of men and women in Christ Jesus.

As the flower turns to the sun, that the bright beams may aid in perfecting its beauty and symmetry, so should we turn to the Sun of Righteousness, that heaven's light may shine upon us, that our character may be developed into the likeness of Christ.

Jesus teaches the same thing when He says, "Abide in Me, and I in you. As the branch cannot bear fruit of itself, except it abide in the vine; no more can ye, except ye abide in Me. . . . Without Me ye can do nothing." John 15:4, 5. You are just as dependent upon Christ, in order to live a holy life, as is the branch upon the parent stock for growth and fruitfulness. Apart from Him you have no life. You have no power to resist temptation or to grow in grace and holiness. Abiding in Him, you may flourish. Drawing your life from Him, you will not wither nor be fruitless. You will be like a tree planted by the rivers of water.

(24) Many have an idea that they must do some part of the work alone. They have trusted in Christ for the forgiveness of sin, but now they seek by their own efforts to live aright. But every such effort must fail. Jesus says, "Without Me ye can do nothing." Our growth in grace, our joy, our usefulness,—all depend upon our union with Christ. It is by communion with Him, daily, hourly,—by abiding in Him,—that we are to grow in grace. He is not only the Author, but the Finisher of our faith. It is Christ first and last and always. He is to be with us, not only at the beginning and the end of our course, but at every step of the

way. David says, "I have set the Lord always before me: because He is at my right hand, I shall not be moved." Psalm 16:8.

Do you ask, "How am I to abide in Christ?" In the same way as you received Him at first. "As ye have therefore received Christ Jesus the Lord, so walk ye in Him." "The just shall live by faith." Colossians 2:6; Hebrews 10:38. You gave yourself to God, to be His wholly, to serve and obey Him, and you took Christ as your Saviour. You could not yourself atone for your sins or change your

DEPENDENCE ON GOD

SAVED FROM THE SUBTERRANEAN

Gary Lutes and his sons, Buddy and Tim, had entered New Trout Cave near Franklin, West Virginia, and were exploring an area known as "The Maze" when they came to a sharp drop-off. Gary decided to leave behind the pack with the emergency lighting, food, and water.

Ten minutes later and 200 feet deeper in the cave, as Tim's light began to dim, they turned around to head back. Then Tim's light went out. And Buddy's. Everything looked the same. Then Gary's light went out. There they stayed—lost, tired, hungry, and thirsty—until five days later, when a rescue party found them.

Like Gary, Buddy, and Tim, we often trust our instincts in making decisions every day. Take a look in the indicated paragraph (see 24 on page 70) and see how important it is to be completely dependent on God.

- If you were a caver, how would dependence on God figure in your cave exploration?
- How dependent are you on God? Do you pray to Him when things are going good, going bad, and at other times?

CONSIDER...

- praying to God and asking Him to help you depend on Him.
- making a "text tree." Use a concordance to find Bible texts from words such as *trust, guide, lead, help,* etc. Decide which texts speak the clearest to you, put them in groups (like branches) and in order of importance (like a tree trunk). Mount the tree on your wall or door.

FOR MORE, SEE...

- Joshua 1:9
- 1 Kings 3:5-15
- Proverbs 3:5, 6
- Isaiah 26:3, 4

—KP

heart; but having given yourself to God, you believe that He for Christ's sake did all this for you. By *faith* you became Christ's, and by faith you are to grow up in Him—by giving and taking. You are to *give* all,—your heart, your will, your service,—give yourself to Him to obey all His requirements; and you must *take* all,—Christ, the fullness of all blessing, to abide in your heart, to be your strength, your righteousness, your everlasting helper,—to give you power to obey.

Consecrate yourself to God in the morning; make this your very first work. Let your prayer be, "Take me, O Lord, as wholly Thine. I lay all my plans at Thy feet. Use me today in Thy service. Abide with me, and let all my work be wrought in Thee." This is a daily matter. Each morning consecrate yourself to God for that day. Surrender all your plans to Him, to be carried out or given up as His providence shall indicate. Thus day by day you may be giving your life into the hands of God, and thus your life will be molded more and more after the life of Christ.

A life in Christ is a life of restfulness. There may be no ecstasy of feeling, but there should be an abiding, peaceful trust. Your hope is not in yourself; it is in Christ. Your weakness is united to His strength, your ignorance to His wisdom, your frailty to His enduring might. So you are not to look to yourself, not to let the mind dwell upon self, but look to Christ. Let the mind dwell upon His love, upon the beauty, the perfection, of His character. Christ in His self-denial, Christ in His humiliation, Christ in His purity and holiness, Christ in His matchless love—this is the subject for the soul's contemplation. It is by loving Him, copying Him, depending wholly upon Him, that you are to be transformed into His likeness.

Jesus says, "Abide in Me." These words convey the idea of rest, stability, confidence. Again He invites,"Come unto Me, . . . and I will give you rest." Matthew 11:28. The words of the psalmist express the same thought: "Rest in the Lord, and wait patiently for Him." And Isaiah gives the assurance, "In quietness and in confidence shall be your strength." Psalm 37:7; Isaiah 30:15. This rest is not found in inactivity; for in the Saviour's invitation the promise of rest is united with the call to labor: "Take My yoke upon you: . . . and ye shall find rest."Matthew 11:29. The heart that rests most fully upon Christ will be most earnest and active in labor for Him.

(25) When the mind dwells upon self, it is turned away from Christ, the source of strength and life. Hence it is Satan's constant effort to keep the attention diverted from the Saviour and thus prevent the union and communion of the soul with Christ. The pleasures of the world, life's cares and perplexities and sorrows, the faults of others, or your own faults and imperfections—to any or all of these he will seek to divert the mind. Do not be misled by his devices. Many who are really conscientious, and who desire to live for God, he too often leads to dwell upon their own faults and weaknesses, and thus by separating them from Christ he hopes to gain the victory. We should not make self the center and indulge anxiety and fear as to whether we shall be saved. All this turns the soul away from the Source of our strength. Commit the keeping of your soul to God, and trust in Him. Talk and think of Jesus. Let self be lost in Him. Put away all doubt; dismiss your fears. Say with the apostle Paul, "I live; yet not I, but Christ liveth in me: and the life which I now live in the flesh I live by the faith of the Son of God, who loved me, and gave Himself for me." Galatians 2:20. Rest in God. He is able to keep that which you have committed to Him. If you will

When the mind dwells upon self, it is turned away from Christ, the source of strength and life.

leave yourself in His hands, He will bring you off more than conqueror through Him that has loved you.

When Christ took human nature upon Him, He bound humanity to Himself by a tie of love that can never be broken by any power save the choice of man himself. Satan will constantly

D I S T R A C T I O N S

MAZEPOVA'S MASTERPIECE

At age 67 Galina Mazepova submitted a 477-page doctoral thesis to the Russian Academy of Sciences. Two aspects of her thesis are worth noting. First, the subject—a species of crayfish 1.5 mm long that lives on the bottom of Lake Baikal in Siberia. Second, the time it took for her research—24 years. Mazepova declares that she will continue studying this crayfish for the rest of her life.

It's hard to think of anything more insignificant than this tiny crustacean sitting in its shell in a remote Siberian lake.

What dedication and powers of concentration Mazepova must have had. Surely there were times during those long years when she was tempted to change her topic. At the least she might have broadened her research to study the whole lake! But nothing could distract her from the task.

Unlike Mazepova, most of us are easily distracted. Even from far more important things than a tiny crayfish. Consider, for example, all the distractions that stop us from keeping our focus on Jesus. The indicated paragraph (see 25 on page 73) suggests ways to combat these distractions.

- What do you think would eventually crop up in any conversation with Galina Mazepova? Is there a lesson in this for Christians?
- What things distract you most from Jesus?

CONSIDER...

- evaluating your typical weekly calendar. How much time do you regularly set aside to focus on Jesus and spiritual things?
- memorizing a portion of Scripture that helps you concentrate on Jesus and His love.

FOR MORE, SEE...

- Matthew 14:22-33
- Mark 4:13, 18
- 2 Corinthians 4:16-18

—GK

present allurements to induce us to break this tie—to choose to separate ourselves from Christ. Here is where we need to watch, to strive, to pray, that nothing may entice us to *choose* another master; for we are always free to do this. But let us keep our eyes fixed upon Christ, and He will preserve us. Looking unto Jesus, we are safe. Nothing can pluck us out of His hand. In constantly beholding Him, we "are changed into the same image from glory to glory, even as by the Spirit of the Lord." 2 Corinthians 3:18.

It was thus that the early disciples gained their likeness to the dear Saviour. When those disciples heard the words of Jesus, they felt their need of Him. They sought, they found, they followed Him. They were with Him in the house, at the table, in the closet, in the field. They were with Him as pupils with a teacher, daily receiving from His lips lessons of holy truth. They looked to Him, as servants to their master, to learn their duty. Those disciples were men "subject to like passions as we are." James 5:17. They had the same battle with sin to fight. They needed the same grace, in order to live a holy life.

Even John, the beloved disciple, the one who most fully reflected the likeness of the Saviour, did not naturally possess that loveliness of character. He was not only self-assertive and ambitious for honor, but impetuous, and resentful under injuries. But as the character of the Divine One was manifested to him, he saw his own deficiency and was humbled by the knowledge. The strength and patience, the power and tenderness, the majesty and meekness, that he beheld in the daily life of the Son of God, filled his soul with admiration and love. Day by day his heart was drawn out toward Christ, until he lost sight of self in love for his Master. His resentful, ambitious temper was yielded to the molding power of Christ. The regenerating influence of the Holy Spirit renewed his heart. The power of the love of Christ wrought a transformation of character. This is the sure result of union with

Jesus. When Christ abides in the heart, the whole nature is transformed. Christ's Spirit, His love, softens the heart, subdues the soul, and raises the thoughts and desires toward God and heaven.

When Christ ascended to heaven, the sense of His presence was still with His followers. It was a personal presence, full of love and light. Jesus, the Saviour, who had walked and talked and prayed with them, who had spoken hope and comfort to their hearts, had, while the message of peace was still upon His lips, been taken up from them into heaven, and the tones of His voice had come back to them, as the cloud of angels received Him—"Lo, I am with you alway, even unto the end of the world." Matthew 28:20. He had ascended to heaven in the form of humanity. They knew that He was before the throne of God, their Friend and Saviour still; that His sympathies were unchanged; that He was still identified with suffering humanity. He was presenting before God the merits of His own precious blood, showing His wounded hands and feet, in remembrance of the price He had paid for His redeemed. They knew that He had ascended to heaven to prepare places for them, and that He would come again and take them to Himself.

When Christ abides in the heart, the whole nature is transformed.

As they met together after the ascension they were eager to present their requests to the Father in the name of Jesus. In solemn awe they bowed in prayer, repeating the assurance, "Whatsoever ye shall ask the Father in My name, He will give it you. Hitherto have ye asked nothing in My name: ask, and ye shall receive, that your joy may be full." John 16:23, 24. They extended the hand of faith higher and higher with the mighty argument, "It is Christ that died, yea rather, that is risen again, who is even at the right hand of God, who also maketh intercession for us." Romans 8:34. And Pentecost brought them the presence of the Comforter, of whom Christ had said, He "shall be in you." And He had further said, "It is expedient for you that I go away: for if I go not away, the Comforter will not come unto you; but if I depart, I will send Him unto you." John 14:17; 16:7. Henceforth through the Spirit, Christ was to abide continually in the hearts of His children. Their union with Him was closer than when He was personally with them. The light, and love, and power of the indwelling Christ shone out through them, so that men, beholding, "marveled; and they took knowledge of them, that they had been with Jesus." Acts 4:13.

All that Christ was to the disciples, He desires to be to His children today; for in that last prayer, with the little band of disciples gathered about Him, He said, "Neither pray I for these alone, but for them also which shall believe on Me through their word." John 17:20.

Jesus prayed for us, and He asked that we might be one with Him, even as He is one with the Father. What a union is this! The Saviour has said of Himself, "The Son can do nothing of Himself;" "the Father that dwelleth in Me, He doeth the works." John 5:19; 14:10. Then if Christ is dwelling in our hearts, He will work in us "both to will and to do of His good pleasure." Philippians 2:13. We shall work as He worked; we shall manifest the same spirit. And thus, loving Him and abiding in Him, we shall "grow up into Him in all things, which is the head, even Christ." Ephesians 4:15.

THE WORK AND THE LIFE

God is the source of life and light and joy to the universe. Like rays of light from the sun, like the streams of water bursting from a living spring, blessings flow out from Him to all His creatures. And wherever the life of God is in the hearts of men, it will flow out to others in love and blessing.

Our Saviour's joy was in the uplifting and redemption of fallen men. For this He counted not His life dear unto Himself, but endured the cross, despising the shame. So angels are ever engaged in working for the happiness of others. This is their joy. That which selfish hearts would regard as humiliating service, ministering to those who are wretched and in every way inferior in character and rank, is the work of sinless angels. The spirit of Christ's self-sacrificing love is the spirit that pervades heaven and is the very essence of its bliss. This is the spirit that Christ's followers will possess, the work that they will do.

When the love of Christ is enshrined in the heart, like sweet fragrance it cannot be hidden. Its holy influence will be felt by all with whom we come in contact. The spirit of Christ in the heart is like a spring in the desert, flowing to refresh all and making those who are ready to perish, eager to drink of the water of life.

Love to Jesus will be manifested in a desire to work as He worked for the blessing and uplifting of humanity. It will lead to love, tenderness, and sympathy toward all the creatures of our heavenly Father's care.

The Saviour's life on earth was not a life of ease and devotion to Himself, but He toiled with persistent, earnest, untiring effort for the salvation of lost mankind. From the manger to

Calvary He followed the path of self-denial and sought not to be released from arduous tasks, painful travels and exhausting care and labor. He said, "The Son of man came not to be ministered unto, but to minister, and to give His life a ransom for many." Matthew 20:28. This was the one great object of His life. Everything else was secondary and subservient. It was His meat and drink to do the will of God and to finish His work. Self and self-interest had no part in His labor.

So those who are the partakers of the grace of Christ will be ready to make any sacrifice, that others for whom He died may share the heavenly gift. They will do all they can to make the world better for their stay in it. This spirit is the sure outgrowth of a soul truly converted. No sooner does one come to Christ than there is born in his heart a desire to make known to others what a precious friend he has found in Jesus; the saving and sanctifying truth cannot be shut up in his heart. If we are clothed with the righteousness of Christ and are filled with the joy of His indwelling Spirit, we shall not be able to hold our peace. If we have tasted and seen that the Lord is good we shall have something to tell. Like Philip when he found the Saviour, we shall invite others into His presence. We shall seek to present to them the attractions of Christ and the unseen realities of the world to come. There will be an intensity of desire to follow in the path that Jesus trod. There will be an earnest longing that those around us may "behold the Lamb of God, which taketh away the sin of the world." John 1:29.

When the love of Christ is enshrined in the heart, like sweet fragrance it cannot be hidden.

26 And the effort to bless others will react in blessings upon ourselves. This was the purpose of God in giving us a part to act

in the plan of redemption. He has granted men the privilege of becoming partakers of the divine nature and, in their turn, of diffusing blessings to their fellow men. This is the highest honor, the greatest joy, that it is possible for God to bestow upon men. Those who thus become participants in labors of love are brought nearest to their Creator.

God might have committed the message of the gospel, and all the work of loving ministry, to the heavenly angels. He might

HELPING OTHERS

THE CAN MAN CAN!

Ebb Clarence Aaby is 100 years old, and 100-percent active.

Every day the 4-foot-11-inch can man walks nearly three miles on foot to collect aluminum cans. He carries a hooked ski-pole "retriever" to search through local dumpsters in College Place, Washington, where he lives.

Standing on tip-toe, Ebb is just tall enough to peer over the edge of garbage bins that are almost always overflowing with smelly garbage. He uses his retriever to pull the sticky cans from the bins and drop them one by one into the plastic garbage sack that he hauls around with him.

Why does he do it? He believes in helping others, no matter the cost. He uses the money he makes from recycling the cans to help students get a Christian education.

Ebb sees his sacrifice as coming back to him by seeing others happy. Jesus helps us feel good inside about helping others. That's partly why we love to do it so much. Read the indicated paragraph (see 26 on page 79) to discover how helping others really helps us.

- What returns make sacrificing worthwhile to Ebb?
- When do you most feel you are living your life to the fullest?

CONSIDER...

- interviewing a member of your church who you think has shown that he or she enjoys serving others. Ask how you may get involved in such an activity.
- sacrificing one hour today that you'd spend on yourself to help someone else.

FOR MORE, SEE...

- Psalm 41:1-3
- Matthew 25:34-40
- Luke 6:38

—LC

have employed other means for accomplishing His purpose. But in His infinite love He chose to make us co-workers with Himself, with Christ and the angels, that we might share the blessing, the joy, the spiritual uplifting, which results from this unselfish ministry.

We are brought into sympathy with Christ through the fellowship of His sufferings. Every act of self-sacrifice for the good of others strengthens the spirit of beneficence in the giver's heart, allying him more closely to the Redeemer of the world, who "was rich, yet for your sakes . . . became poor, that ye through His poverty might be rich." 2 Corinthians 8:9. And it is only as we thus fulfill the divine purpose in our creation that life can be a blessing to us.

If you will go to work as Christ designs that His disciples shall, and win souls for Him, you will feel the need of a deeper experience and a greater knowledge in divine things, and will hunger and thirst after righteousness. You will plead with God, and your faith will be strengthened, and your soul will drink deeper drafts at the well of salvation. Encountering opposition and trials will drive you to the Bible and prayer. You will grow in grace and the knowledge of Christ, and will develop a rich experience.

The spirit of unselfish labor for others gives depth, stability, and Christlike loveliness to the character, and brings peace and happiness to its possessor. The aspirations are elevated. There is no room for sloth or selfishness. Those who thus exercise the Christian graces will grow and will become strong to work for God. They will have clear spiritual perceptions, a steady, growing faith, and an increased power in prayer. The Spirit of God, moving upon their spirit, calls forth the sacred harmonies of the soul in answer to the divine touch. Those who thus devote themselves to unselfish effort for the good of others are most surely working out their own salvation.

The only way to grow in grace is to be disinterestedly doing the very work which Christ has enjoined upon us—to engage, to the extent of our ability, in helping and blessing those who need the help we can give them. Strength comes by exercise; activity is the very condition of life.

The greater part of our Saviour's life on earth was spent in patient toil in the carpenter's shop at Nazareth.

Those who endeavor to maintain Christian life by passively accepting the blessings that come through the means of grace, and doing nothing for Christ, are simply trying to live by eating without working. And in the spiritual as in the natural world, this always results in degeneration and decay. A man who would refuse to exercise his limbs would soon lose all power to use them. Thus the Christian who will not exercise his God-given powers not only fails to grow up into Christ, but he loses the strength that he already had.

The church of Christ is God's appointed agency for the salvation of men. Its mission is to carry the gospel to the world. And the obligation rests upon all Christians. Everyone, to the extent of his talent and opportunity, is to fulfill the Saviour's commission. The love of Christ, revealed to us, makes us debtors to all who know Him not. God has given us light, not for ourselves alone, but to shed upon them.

If the followers of Christ were awake to duty, there would be thousands where there is one today proclaiming the gospel in heathen lands. And all who could not personally engage in the work, would yet sustain it with their means, their sympathy, and their prayers. And there would be far more earnest labor for souls in Christian countries.

We need not go to heathen lands, or even leave the narrow circle of the home, if it is there that our duty lies, in order to work for Christ. We can do this in the home circle, in the church, among those with whom we associate, and with whom we do business. The greater part of our Saviour's life on earth was spent in patient toil in the carpenter's shop at Nazareth. Ministering angels attended the Lord of life as He walked side by side with peasants and laborers, unrecognized and unhonored. He was as faithfully fulfilling His mission while working at His humble trade as when He healed the sick or walked upon the storm-tossed waves of Galilee. So in the humblest duties and lowliest positions of life, we may walk and work with Jesus.

The apostle says, "Let every man, wherein he is called, therein abide with God." 1 Corinthians 7:24. The businessman may conduct his business in a way that will glorify his Master because of his fidelity. If he is a true follower of Christ he will carry his religion into everything that is done and reveal to men the spirit of Christ. The mechanic may be a diligent and faithful representative of Him who toiled in the lowly walks of life among the hills of Galilee. Everyone who names the name of Christ should so work that others, by seeing his good works, may be led to glorify their Creator and Redeemer.

[27] Many have excused themselves from rendering their gifts to the service of Christ because others were possessed of superior endowments and advantages. The opinion has prevailed that only those who are especially talented are required to consecrate their abilities to the service of God. It has come to be understood by many that talents are given to only a certain favored class to the exclusion of others who of course are not called upon to share in the toils or the rewards. But it is not so represented in the parable. When the master of the house called his servants, he gave to every man *his* work.

With a loving spirit we may perform life's humblest duties "as to the Lord." Colossians 3:23. If the love of God is in the heart, it will be manifested in the life. The sweet savor of Christ will surround us, and our influence will elevate and bless.

You are not to wait for great occasions or to expect extraordinary abilities before you go to work for God. You need not have a thought of what the world will think of you. If your daily life is a testimony to the purity and sincerity of your faith,

T A L E N T S

ALBERT'S ABILITIES

Albert is a very poor student," read the teacher's report. "He is mentally slow, unsociable, and is always daydreaming. He is spoiling it for the rest of the class. It would be in the best interest of all if he were removed from school at once."

Despite this unfavorable report, young Albert stayed in school. Eventually he finished school, went on to college, and began a successful career as a scientist. Years later, a minister wrote a letter to a group of the world's leading scientists. He asked each to list the 14 greatest scientists of all time. When the lists came back, no two were alike. Nevertheless, one name appeared on all 14 lists—Albert Einstein, the same Albert who was described many years before as "a very poor student" and "mentally slow."

God gave Albert Einstein a great talent. God gives everyone unique abilities. Read the indicated paragraph (see 27 on page 83) to see how God values your special talent.

- Have you discovered what your special talent is?
- What difference could you make in this world if you were to make the most of your talent?

CONSIDER...

- making a list of all the things you really like to do—then underline those activities you could excel at if you really worked at it.
- asking your parent, your best friend, and your favorite teacher what they think your special talent is.

FOR MORE, SEE...

- Matthew 25:14-30
- Romans 12:6-8
- 1 Corinthians 3:5-9

—CD

and others are convinced that you desire to benefit them, your efforts will not be wholly lost.

The humblest and poorest of the disciples of Jesus can be a blessing to others. They may not realize that they are doing any special good, but by their unconscious influence they may start waves of blessing that will widen and deepen, and the blessed results they may never know until the day of final reward. They do not feel or know that they are doing anything great. They are not required to weary themselves with anxiety about success. They have only to go forward quietly, doing faithfully the work that God's providence assigns, and their life will not be in vain. Their own souls will be growing more and more into the likeness of Christ; they are workers together with God in this life and are thus fitting for the higher work and the unshadowed joy of the life to come.

With a loving spirit we may perform life's humblest duties "as to the Lord."

A KNOWLEDGE OF GOD

Many are the ways in which God is seeking to make Himself known to us and bring us into communion with Him. Nature speaks to our senses without ceasing. The open heart will be impressed with the love and glory of God as revealed through the works of His hands. The listening ear can hear and understand the communications of God through the things of nature. The green fields, the lofty trees, the buds and flowers, the passing cloud, the falling rain, the babbling brook, the glories of the heavens, speak to our hearts, and invite us to become acquainted with Him who made them all.

Our Saviour bound up His precious lessons with the things of nature. The trees, the birds, the flowers of the valleys, the hills, the lakes, and the beautiful heavens, as well as the incidents and surroundings of daily life, were all linked with the words of truth, that His lessons might thus be often recalled to mind, even amid the busy cares of man's life of toil.

God would have His children appreciate His works and delight in the simple, quiet beauty with which He has adorned our earthly home. He is a lover of the beautiful, and above all that is outwardly attractive He loves beauty of character; He would have us cultivate purity and simplicity, the quiet graces of the flowers. If we will but listen, God's created works will teach us precious lessons of obedience and trust.

From the stars that in their trackless courses through space follow from age to age their appointed path, down to the minutest atom, the things of nature obey the Creator's will. And God cares for everything and sustains everything that He has created. He who upholds the unnumbered worlds throughout immensity, at the same time cares for the wants of the little brown sparrow that sings its humble song without fear. When men go forth to their daily toil, as when they engage in prayer; when they lie down at night, and when they rise in the morning; when the rich man feasts in his palace, or when the poor man gathers his children about the scanty board, each is tenderly watched by the heavenly Father. No tears are shed that God does not notice. There is no smile that He does not mark.

If we would but fully believe this, all undue anxieties would be dismissed. Our lives would not be so filled with disappointment as now; for everything, whether great or small, would be left in the hands of God, who is not perplexed by the multiplicity of cares, or overwhelmed by their weight. We should then enjoy a rest of soul to which many have long been strangers.

As your senses delight in the attractive loveliness of the earth, think of the world that is to come, that shall never know the blight of sin and death; where the face of nature will no more wear the shadow of the curse. Let your imagination picture the home of the saved, and remember that it will be more glorious than your brightest imagination can portray. In the varied gifts of God in nature we see but the faintest gleaming of His glory. It is written, "Eye hath not seen, nor ear heard, neither have entered into the heart of man, the things which God hath prepared for them that love Him." 1 Corinthians 2:9.

If we will but listen, God's created works will teach us precious lessons of obedience and trust.

The poet and the naturalist have many things to say about nature, but it is the Christian who enjoys the beauty of the earth with the highest appreciation, because he recognizes his Father's handiwork and perceives His love in flower and shrub and tree. No one can fully appreciate the significance of hill and vale, river and sea, who does not look upon them as an expression of God's love to man.

(28) God speaks to us through His providential workings and through the influence of His Spirit upon the heart. In our

HEARING GOD

MYSTERY OF THE WHEEL

For centuries certain Native North American landmarks have remained a mystery to Western society. What were these strange stone circles and squares laid out on the ground? Ancient religious relics? Medicine man magic? Part of a ceremonial rite?

One of these mysteries lies atop a Wyoming plateau. A circle of stones surrounds a pile of stones at its center, and 28 lines of stones radiate from the pile like spokes in a wheel. In the early 1970s astronomer John Eddy finally "broke the code." By standing at certain points on the wheel, he learned that the stones carefully marked sunrise and sunset on the longest day of the year and charted stars visible just before and after the summer solstice. The wheel was really a calendar built by astronomers centuries ago! The Native Americans probably used this observatory to determine when to assemble for summer trading fairs.

By observing patterns in our lives, understanding how God works, and aligning ourselves with biblical truths, we can translate some of life's "mysteries" into logical, divine messages. Study the indicated paragraph (see (28) on page 88) to learn the importance of spiritual observation.

- What qualities would you need as an ancient astronomer? As a teenager searching for God's will?
- Where and how can you hear God's voice?

CONSIDER...

- looking at the stars tonight. How do they make you feel about being a child of God?
- making a list of "turning points" in your life. What patterns do you see?

FOR MORE, SEE...

- Genesis 45:4-8
- Job 11:7-20
- Psalm 37

—BK

circumstances and surroundings, in the changes daily taking place around us, we may find precious lessons if our hearts are but open to discern them. The psalmist, tracing the work of God's providence, says, "The earth is full of the goodness of the Lord." "Whoso is wise, and will observe these things, even they shall understand the loving-kindness of the Lord." Psalm 33:5; 107:43.

God speaks to us in His word. Here we have in clearer lines the revelation of His character, of His dealings with men, and the great work of redemption. Here is open before us the history of patriarchs and prophets and other holy men of old. They were men "subject to like passions as we are." James 5:17. We see how they struggled through discouragements like our own, how they fell under temptation as we have done, and yet took heart again and conquered through the grace of God; and, beholding, we are encouraged in our striving after righteousness. As we read of the precious experiences granted them, of the light and love and blessing it was theirs to enjoy, and of the work they wrought through the grace given them, the spirit that inspired them kindles a flame of holy emulation in our hearts and a desire to be like them in character—like them to walk with God.

If you would become acquainted with the Saviour, study the Holy Scriptures.

Jesus said of the Old Testament Scriptures,—and how much more is it true of the New,—"They are they which testify of Me," the Redeemer, Him in whom our hopes of eternal life are centered. John 5:39. Yes, the whole Bible tells of Christ. From the first record of creation—for "without Him was not anything made that was made"—to the closing promise, "Behold, I come quickly," we are reading of His works and listening to His voice.

John 1:3; Revelation 22:12. If you would become acquainted with the Saviour, study the Holy Scriptures.

Fill the whole heart with the words of God. They are the living water, quenching your burning thirst. They are the living bread from heaven. Jesus declares, "Except ye eat the flesh of the Son of man, and drink His blood, ye have no life in you." And He explains Himself by saying, "The words that I speak unto you, they are spirit, and they are life." John 6:53, 63. Our bodies are built up from what we eat and drink; and as in the natural economy, so in the spiritual economy: it is what we meditate upon that will give tone and strength to our spiritual nature.

The Bible was not written for the scholar alone; on the contrary, it was designed for the common people.

The theme of redemption is one that the angels desire to look into; it will be the science and the song of the redeemed throughout the ceaseless ages of eternity. Is it not worthy of careful thought and study now? The infinite mercy and love of Jesus, the sacrifice made in our behalf, call for the most serious and solemn reflection. We should dwell upon the character of our dear Redeemer and Intercessor. We should meditate upon the mission of Him who came to save His people from their sins. As we thus contemplate heavenly themes, our faith and love will grow stronger, and our prayers will be more and more acceptable to God, because they will be more and more mixed with faith and love. They will be intelligent and fervent. There will be more constant confidence in Jesus, and a daily, living experience in His power to save to the uttermost all that come unto God by Him.

As we meditate upon the perfections of the Saviour, we shall desire to be wholly transformed and renewed in the image of His purity. There will be a hungering and thirsting of soul to become like Him whom we adore. The more our thoughts are upon Christ, the more we shall speak of Him to others and represent Him to the world.

The Bible was not written for the scholar alone; on the contrary, it was designed for the common people. The great truths necessary for salvation are made as clear as noonday; and none will mistake and lose their way except those who follow their own judgment instead of the plainly revealed will of God.

We should not take the testimony of any man as to what the Scriptures teach, but should study the words of God for ourselves. If we allow others to do our thinking, we shall have crippled energies and contracted abilities. The noble powers of the mind may be so dwarfed by lack of exercise on themes worthy of their concentration as to lose their ability to grasp the deep meaning of the word of God. The mind will enlarge if it is employed in tracing out the relation of the subjects of the Bible, comparing scripture with scripture and spiritual things with spiritual.

(29) There is nothing more calculated to strengthen the intellect than the study of the Scriptures. No other book is so potent to elevate the thoughts, to give vigor to the faculties, as the broad, ennobling truths of the Bible. If God's word were studied as it should be, men would have a breadth of mind, a nobility of character, and a stability of purpose rarely seen in these times.

But there is but little benefit derived from a hasty reading of the Scriptures. One may read the whole Bible through and yet fail to see its beauty or comprehend its deep and hidden meaning. One passage studied until its significance is clear to the mind and its relation to the plan of salvation is evident, is of more value than the perusal of many chapters with no definite purpose in view and no positive instruction gained. Keep your Bible with you. As you have opportunity, read it; fix the texts in your memory. Even while you are walking the streets you may read a passage and meditate upon it, thus fixing it in the mind.

(30) We cannot obtain wisdom without earnest attention and prayerful study. Some portions of Scripture are indeed too plain to be misunderstood, but there are others whose meaning does not lie on the surface to be seen at a glance. Scripture must be compared with scripture. There must be careful research and prayerful reflection. And such study will be richly repaid. As the

INTELLIGENCE

BUT IS HE COOL?

Scott was nearly 15 and his passion was cars. His friends called him "Mr. Mechanic." It was his dream to build his own car by the time he got his driver's license. That would be cool!

Scott was so busy reading up on the latest race results and talking to his friends about the latest model cars that he didn't have much time to visit his retired neighbor. "Old guys just aren't that cool." That seemed to be Scott's attitude until he found out that old Mr. Gutierrez used to design cars. Scott realized that Mr. Gutierrez could teach him things that no one else could.

Scott found that a car designer could help him with his interest far more than all the other sources he'd been consulting. The indicated paragraph (see (29) on page 91) says that the Bible, a book by our Designer, can help us far more than all the other sources of "wisdom" competing for our attention.

- Why do we sometimes overlook the Bible as a source of intellectual improvement?
- How could Bible study "strengthen the intellect"?

CONSIDER...

- setting aside 10 minutes every day to study your favorite topic in the Bible.
- comparing your favorite TV show or book to what the Bible says about the same subject.

FOR MORE, SEE...

- Psalm 111:10
- Ecclesiastes 1:13, 14; 2:26
- John 1:1-5
- James 1:5; 3:17

—PC

miner discovers veins of precious metal concealed beneath the surface of the earth, so will he who perseveringly searches the word of God as for hid treasure find truths of the greatest value, which are concealed from the view of the careless seeker. The words of inspiration, pondered in the heart, will be as streams flowing from the fountain of life.

B I B L E S T U D Y

WHAT A FIND!

On June 12, 1971, Don Kincaid, a 25-year-old diver and underwater photographer, jumped into the water off Key West, Florida. Near the bottom he came upon something gold sticking out of the sand.

"I just grabbed," he remembers. "It was a chain of some kind. In the green light, it looked like cheap brass.

Kincaid, a member of a team of treasure hunters, had come upon part of the wreck of the *Nuestra Senora de Atocha*, a Spanish galleon that sank in the Florida Keys in 1622. For 20 years the team had been searching for the sunken ship.

Even after this first discovery it took them years to find the rest of the treasure. It had been scattered over 12 miles, some of it beneath 20 feet of water and 20 more feet of sand. When they had finally brought all the gold, silver, emeralds, and artifacts to the surface, it amounted to 400 million dollars' worth.

Have you ever thought of the Bible as a sea filled with buried treasure? The indicated paragraph (see 30 on page 92) tells how, through prayerful and careful study, you can uncover information about God.

- How is Bible study like Don Kincaid's treasure hunt?
- How has the Bible changed your life?

CONSIDER...

- opening your Bible and memorizing an encouraging text.
- underlining in bright colors Bible passages that are meaningful to you. Write your questions and reactions in the margins. Make your Bible a conversation between you and God.

FOR MORE, SEE...

- Psalm 119
- Matthew 4:4
- Luke 6:46-49
- 2 Timothy 3:10-17

—LP

Never should the Bible be studied without prayer. Before opening its pages we should ask for the enlightenment of the Holy Spirit, and it will be given. When Nathanael came to Jesus, the Saviour exclaimed, "Behold an Israelite indeed, in whom is no guile!" Nathanael said, "Whence knowest Thou me?" Jesus answered, "Before that Philip called thee, when thou wast under the fig tree, I saw thee." John 1:47, 48. And Jesus will see us also in the secret places of prayer if we will seek Him for light that we may know what is truth. Angels from the world of light will be with those who in humility of heart seek for divine guidance.

The Holy Spirit exalts and glorifies the Saviour. It is His office to present Christ, the purity of His righteousness, and the great salvation that we have through Him. Jesus says, "He shall receive of Mine, and shall show it unto you." John 16:14. The Spirit of truth is the only effectual teacher of divine truth. How must God esteem the human race, since He gave His Son to die for them and appoints His Spirit to be man's teacher and continual guide!

THE PRIVILEGE OF PRAYER

Through nature and revelation, through His providence, and by the influence of His Spirit, God speaks to us. But these are not enough; we need also to pour out our hearts to Him. In order to have spiritual life and energy, we must have an actual relationship with our heavenly Father. Our minds may be drawn out toward Him; we may meditate upon His works, His mercies, His blessings; but this is not, in the fullest sense, communing with Him. In order to commune with God, we must have something to say to Him concerning our actual life.

Prayer is the opening of the heart to God as to a friend. Not that it is necessary in order to make known to God what we are, but in order to enable us to receive Him. Prayer does not bring God down to us, but brings us up to Him.

When Jesus was upon the earth, He taught His disciples how to pray. He directed them to present their daily needs before God, and to cast all their care upon Him. And the assurance He gave them that their petitions should be heard, is assurance also to us.

Jesus Himself, while He dwelt among men, was often in prayer. Our Saviour identified Himself with our needs and weakness, in that He became a suppliant, a petitioner, seeking from His Father fresh supplies of strength, that He might come forth braced for duty and trial. He is our example in all things. He is a brother in our infirmities, "in all points tempted like as we are;" but as the sinless one His nature recoiled from evil; He endured struggles and torture of soul in a world of sin. His humanity made prayer a necessity and a privilege. He found comfort and joy in communion with His Father. And if the Saviour of men, the Son of God, felt the need of prayer, how much more should feeble, sinful mortals feel the necessity of fervent, constant prayer.

Our heavenly Father waits to bestow upon us the fullness of His blessing. It is our privilege to drink largely at the fountain of boundless love. What a wonder it is that we pray so little! God is ready and willing to hear the sincere prayer of the humblest of His children, and yet there is much manifest reluctance on our part to make known our wants to God. What can the angels of heaven think of poor helpless human beings, who are subject to temptation, when God's heart of infinite love yearns toward them, ready to give them more than they can ask or think, and yet they pray so little and have so little faith? The angels love to bow before God; they love to be near Him. They regard communion with God as their highest joy; and yet the children of earth, who need so much the help that God only can give, seem satisfied to walk without the light of His Spirit, the companionship of His presence.

Prayer is the opening of the heart to God as to a friend.

The darkness of the evil one encloses those who neglect to pray. The whispered temptations of the enemy entice them to sin; and it is all because they do not make use of the privileges that God has given them in the divine appointment of prayer. Why should the sons and daughters of God be reluctant to pray, when prayer is the key in the hand of faith to unlock heaven's storehouse, where are treasured the boundless resources of Omnipotence? Without unceasing prayer and diligent watching we are in danger of growing careless and of deviating from the right path. The adversary seeks continually to obstruct the way to the mercy seat, that we may not by earnest supplication and faith obtain grace and power to resist temptation.

There are certain conditions upon which we may expect that God will hear and answer our prayers. One of the first of these is that we feel our need of help from Him. He has promised, "I will pour water upon him that is thirsty, and floods upon the dry ground." Isaiah 44:3. Those who hunger and thirst after righteousness, who long after God, may be sure that they will be filled. The heart must be open to the Spirit's influence, or God's blessing cannot be received.

Our great need is itself an argument and pleads most eloquently in our behalf. But the Lord is to be sought unto to do these things for us. He says, "Ask, and it shall be given you." And "He that spared not His own Son, but delivered Him up for us all, how shall He not with Him also freely give us all things?" Matthew 7:7; Romans 8:32.

If we regard iniquity in our hearts, if we cling to any known sin, the Lord will not hear us; but the prayer of the penitent, contrite soul is always accepted. When all known wrongs are righted, we may believe that God will answer our petitions. Our own merit will never commend us to the favor of God; it is the worthiness of Jesus that will save us, His blood that will cleanse us; yet we have a work to do in complying with the conditions of acceptance.

Another element of prevailing prayer is faith. "He that cometh to God must believe that He is, and that He is a rewarder of them that diligently seek Him." Hebrews 11:6. Jesus said to His disciples, "What things soever ye desire, when ye pray, believe that ye receive them, and ye shall have them." Mark 11:24. Do we take Him at His word?

(31) The assurance is broad and unlimited, and He is faithful who has promised. When we do not receive the very things we

asked for, at the time we ask, we are still to believe that the Lord hears and that He will answer our prayers. We are so erring and shortsighted that we sometimes ask for things that would not be a blessing to us, and our heavenly Father in love answers our prayers by giving us that which will be for our highest good—that which we ourselves would desire if with vision divinely enlightened we could see all things as they really are. When our prayers seem not to be answered, we are to cling to the promise; for the time of

ANSWERS TO PRAYER

RIGHT ON TIME

C. M. Fields was determined to send her six children to church school even though her husband had left her and had refused to help. Each year as registration time approached, she prayed, "Lord, just let me get them in." Every summer she struggled to pay off the previous year's bill before raising money for the next.

Often she didn't know where the money was coming from—or when it would come. Sometimes the children started school late as she gathered the registration fees and tuition. They wore hand-me-downs and ate a limited diet. But they always got in and stayed in.

The yearly experience of getting into school reinforced for C. M.'s children an important lesson she wanted them to learn: "God's answer may not come when you want it, but it's always right on time." Read the indicated paragraph (see 31 on page 97) to see how God works in similar circumstances.

- Why do you think God sometimes waits till the last minute and beyond to answer prayers?
- What is it called when we demand that a prayer be answered in a specific way? Why is that wrong?

CONSIDER...

- discussing with a friend a time when God's answer to a prayer was better than or different from your request.
- listing at least three times when Jesus surprised people with His responses to their requests.

FOR MORE, SEE...

- Psalm 84:11
- Isaiah 55:8, 9
- Jeremiah 29:11

—VF

answering will surely come, and we shall receive the blessing we need most. But to claim that prayer will always be answered in the very way and for the particular thing that we desire, is presumption. God is too wise to err, and too good to withhold any good thing from them that walk uprightly. Then do not fear to trust Him, even though you do not see the immediate answer to your prayers. Rely upon His sure promise, "Ask, and it shall be given you." If we take counsel with our doubts and fears, or try to solve everything that we cannot see clearly, before we have faith, perplexities will only increase and deepen. But if we come to God, feeling helpless and dependent, as we really are, and in humble, trusting faith make known our wants to Him whose knowledge is infinite, who sees everything in creation, and who governs everything by His will and word, He can and will attend to our cry, and will let light shine into our hearts. Through sincere prayer we are brought into connection with the mind of the Infinite. We may have no remarkable evidence at the time that the face of our Redeemer is bending over us in compassion and love, but this is even so. We may not feel His visible touch, but His hand is upon us in love and pitying tenderness.

When we come to ask mercy and blessing from God we should have a spirit of love and forgiveness in our own hearts. How can we pray, "Forgive us our debts, *as* we forgive our debtors," and yet indulge an unforgiving spirit? Matthew 6:12. If we expect our own prayers to be heard we must forgive others in the same manner and to the same extent as we hope to be forgiven.

Perseverance in prayer has been made a condition of receiving. We must pray always if we would grow in faith and experience. We are to be "instant in prayer," to "continue in prayer, and watch in the same with thanksgiving." Romans 12:12; Colossians 4:2. Peter exhorts believers to be "sober, and watch unto prayer." 1 Peter 4:7. Paul directs, "In everything by prayer and supplication with thanksgiving let your requests be made known unto God." Philippians 4:6. "But ye, beloved," says Jude, "praying in the Holy Ghost, keep yourselves in the love of God." Jude 20, 21.

Unceasing prayer is the unbroken union of the soul with God, so that life from God flows into our life; and from our life,

SECRET PRAYER

I ALMOST KILLED HIM

Dr. Ben Carson, the neurosurgeon who performed the first successful separation of Siamese twins joined at the back of the head, remembers in ninth grade trying to knife a friend.

He and Bob were listening to the radio. Bob flipped the dial to another station, and Ben blew up. Grabbing a knife from his back pocket, he snapped it open and lunged for his friend's belly. Miraculously, the knife hit Bob's belt buckle, snapping the blade and falling to the ground.

Ben was shocked. "I–I'm sorry," he muttered to Bob and ran home. There he sank down on the edge of the bathroom tub, weak with the thought that he'd tried to kill his friend. "Lord," Ben prayed, "You have to take this temper from me. If You don't, I'll never be free from it."

After hours of prayer that day, Ben says he hasn't had a problem with temper since. In fact his colleagues call him "Gentle Ben."

Prayer doesn't always work instantly, as in Ben's case, but it is our connection to our heavenly Father, Who can do all things. The indicated paragraph (see (32) on page 101) talks about the strength secret prayer gives us.

- Why do you think Ben's prayer was answered?
- What weakness or temptation do you need God's help in overcoming?

CONSIDER...

- choosing a secret place where you can talk to God.
- recording in a prayer journal the things you pray for and how God answers your prayers.

FOR MORE, SEE...

- Daniel 6
- Jonah 2
- Mark 1:35
- Luke 22:39-46

—LP

purity and holiness flow back to God.

There is necessity for diligence in prayer; let nothing hinder you. Make every effort to keep open the communion between Jesus and your own soul. Seek every opportunity to go where prayer is wont to be made. Those who are really seeking for communion with God will be seen in the prayer meeting, faithful to do their duty and earnest and anxious to reap all the benefits they can gain. They will improve every opportunity of placing themselves where they can receive the rays of light from heaven.

☞32 We should pray in the family circle, and above all we must not neglect secret prayer, for this is the life of the soul. It is impossible for the soul to flourish while prayer is neglected. Family or public prayer alone is not sufficient. In solitude let the soul be laid open to the inspecting eye of God. Secret prayer is to be heard only by the prayer-hearing God. No curious ear is to receive the burden of such petitions. In secret prayer the soul is free from surrounding influences, free from excitement. Calmly, yet fervently, will it reach out after God. Sweet and abiding will be the influence emanating from Him who seeth in secret, whose ear is open to hear the prayer arising from the heart. By calm, simple faith the soul holds communion with God and gathers to itself rays of divine light to strengthen and sustain it in the conflict with Satan. God is our tower of strength.

Pray in your closet, and as you go about your daily labor let your heart be often uplifted to God.

It was thus that Enoch walked with God. These silent prayers rise like precious incense before the throne of grace. Satan cannot overcome him whose heart is thus stayed upon God.

There is no time or place in which it is inappropriate to offer up a petition to God. There is nothing that can prevent us from lifting up our hearts in the spirit of earnest prayer. In the crowds of the street, in the midst of a business engagement, we may send up a petition to God and plead for divine guidance, as did Nehemiah when he made his request before King Artaxerxes. A closet of communion may be found wherever we are. We should have the door of the heart open continually and our invitation going up that Jesus may come and abide as a heavenly guest in the soul.

Although there may be a tainted, corrupted atmosphere around us, we need not breathe its miasma, but may live in the pure air of heaven. We may close every door to impure imaginings and unholy thoughts by lifting the soul into the presence of God through sincere prayer. Those whose hearts are open to receive the support and blessing of God will walk in a holier atmosphere than that of earth and will have constant communion with heaven.

We need to have more distinct views of Jesus and a fuller comprehension of the value of eternal realities. The beauty of holiness is to fill the hearts of God's children; and that this may be accomplished, we should seek for divine disclosures of heavenly things.

Let the soul be drawn out and upward, that God may grant us a breath of the heavenly atmosphere. We may keep so near to God that in every unexpected trial our thoughts will turn to Him as naturally as the flower turns to the sun.

(33) Keep your wants, your joys, your sorrows, your cares, and your fears before God. You cannot burden Him; you cannot weary Him. He who numbers the hairs of your head is not indifferent to the wants of His children. "The Lord is very pitiful, and of tender mercy." James 5:11. His heart of love is touched by our sorrows and even by our utterances of them. Take to Him everything that perplexes the mind. Nothing is too great for Him to bear, for He holds up worlds, He rules over all the affairs of the universe. Nothing that in any way concerns our peace is too small for Him to notice. There is no chapter in our experience too dark for Him to read; there is no perplexity too difficult for Him to unravel. No

calamity can befall the least of His children, no anxiety harass the soul, no joy cheer, no sincere prayer escape the lips, of which our heavenly Father is unobservant, or in which He takes no immediate interest. "He healeth the broken in heart, and bindeth up their wounds." Psalm 147:3. The relations between God and each soul are as distinct and full as though there were not another soul upon the earth to share His watchcare, not another soul for whom He gave His beloved Son.

GOD'S CARE

MISSING THE BOAT

Ann and Lyndelle were fulfilling a dream—cycling in Europe. But part of that dream appeared to be turning into a nightmare. Theo, Ann's friend and their guide, told the girls that there was no way that they could get to Rotterdam on time to catch their boat. Admittedly, this wasn't a matter of life and death, but it threatened to deplete the girls' limited budget and time.

Theo scoffed at the suggestion that they pray, but since they were already late, he didn't object. After the prayer they pressed on and, as Theo had predicted, they arrived late in Rotterdam. When they reached the dock, however, the boat was still there.

Did Theo "miss the boat" because he didn't realize that God is concerned with *every* facet of our lives? The indicated paragraph (see 33 on page 102) says that *nothing* is too big or too small for us to take to God.

- How would you explain to Theo why the boat had not left on time?
- What should you be talking to God about? What's stopping you?

CONSIDER...

- looking up the word *prayer* in a dictionary. How does the definition differ from your own understanding?
- forming a small group of friends to meet once a week to pray for a special need at church or at school.

FOR MORE, SEE...

- 1 Samuel 2:1-10
- Matthew 7:7-11
- Luke 18:1-8
- James 5:16

—PC

Jesus said, "Ye shall ask in My name: and I say not unto you, that I will pray the Father for you: for the Father Himself loveth you." "I have chosen you: . . . that whatsoever ye shall ask of the Father in My name, He may give it you." John 16:26, 27; 15:16. But to pray in the name of Jesus is something more than a mere mention of that name at the beginning and the ending of a prayer. It is to pray in the mind and spirit of Jesus, while we believe His promises, rely upon His grace, and work His works.

God does not mean that any of us should become hermits or monks and retire from the world in order to devote ourselves to acts of worship. The life must be like Christ's life—between the mountain and the multitude. He who does nothing but pray will soon cease to pray, or his prayers will become a formal routine. When men take themselves out of social life, away from the sphere of Christian duty and cross bearing; when they cease to work earnestly for the Master, who worked earnestly for them, they lose the subject matter of prayer and have no incentive to devotion. Their prayers become personal and selfish. They cannot pray in regard to the wants of humanity or the upbuilding of Christ's kingdom, pleading for strength wherewith to work.

(34) We sustain a loss when we neglect the privilege of associating together to strengthen and encourage one another in the service of God. The truths of His word lose their vividness and importance in our minds. Our hearts cease to be enlightened and aroused by their sanctifying influence, and we decline in spirituality. In our association as Christians we lose much by lack of sympathy with one another. He who shuts himself up to himself is not filling the position that God designed he should. The proper cultivation of the social elements in our nature brings us into sympathy with others and is a means of development and strength to us in the service of God.

If Christians would associate together, speaking to each other of the love of God and of the precious truths of redemption, their own hearts would be refreshed and they would refresh one another. We may be daily learning more of our heavenly Father, gaining a fresh experience of His grace; then we shall desire to speak of His love; and as we do this, our own hearts will be warmed and encouraged. If we thought and talked more of Jesus, and less of self, we should have far more of His presence.

CHURCH ATTENDANCE

DOES IT MATTER?

Denise decided to go to church one Sabbath, even though she was sure it wouldn't make a difference to anybody. Hardly had she stepped into the youth room, when a few of the girls introduced themselves. When they discovered she had just moved to the area, they invited her to join them for lunch.

She found the class discussion interesting and lively. Denise felt especially close to Connie, who shared the pain she was experiencing because of her parents' recent divorce. Denise knew all about divorce. She empathized with Connie and gave her some words of encouragement.

As she thought about her near decision not to go to church that day, she realized church attendance *does* matter. It was God's idea to have a special place for you to be able to meet with Him and your friends. That's why He invented church. He's waiting there for you now. The indicated paragraph (see 34 on page 104) describes what we lose when we miss church.

- How do you think Denise's future church attendance could have been affected if she had chosen to stay in bed?
- How can you devote yourself to acts of worship?

CONSIDER...

- seeking out a loner or a visitor at church this Sabbath and making him or her feel glad to have come.
- interviewing several of your friends. Ask them how they feel about church attendance and why.

FOR MORE, SEE...

- Exodus 20:8-11
- Matthew 12:9-13
- 1 Corinthians 3:8, 9

—KB

If we would but think of God as often as we have evidence of His care for us we should keep Him ever in our thoughts and should delight to talk of Him and to praise Him. We talk of temporal things because we have an interest in them. We talk of our friends because we love them; our joys and our sorrows are bound up with them. Yet we have infinitely greater reason to love God than to love our earthly friends; it should be the most natural thing in the world to make Him first in all our thoughts, to talk of His goodness and tell of His power. The rich gifts He has bestowed upon us were not intended to absorb our thoughts and love so much that we should have nothing to give to God; they are constantly to remind us of Him and to bind us in bonds of love and gratitude to our heavenly Benefactor. We dwell too near the lowlands of earth. Let us raise our eyes to the open door of the sanctuary above, where the light of the glory of God shines in the face of Christ, who "is able also to save them to the uttermost that come unto God by Him." Hebrews 7:25.

We need to praise God more "for His goodness, and for His wonderful works to the children of men." Psalm 107:8. Our devotional exercises should not consist wholly in asking and receiving. Let us not be always thinking of our wants and never of the benefits we receive. We do not pray any too much, but we are too sparing of giving thanks. We are the constant recipients of God's mercies, and yet how little gratitude we express, how little we praise Him for what He has done for us.

Anciently the Lord bade Israel, when they met together for His service, "Ye shall eat before the Lord your God, and ye shall rejoice in all that ye put your hand unto, ye and your households, wherein the Lord thy God hath blessed thee." Deuteronomy 12:7. That which is done for the glory of God should be done with cheerfulness, with songs of praise and thanksgiving, not with sadness and gloom.

Our God is a tender, merciful Father. His service should not be looked upon as a heart-saddening, distressing exercise. It should be a pleasure to worship the Lord and to take part in His work. God would not have His children, for whom so great salvation has been provided, act as if He were a hard, exacting taskmaster. He is their best friend; and when they worship Him, He expects to be with them, to bless and comfort them, filling their hearts with joy and love. The Lord desires His children to take comfort in His service and to find more pleasure than hardship in His work. He desires that those who come to worship Him shall carry away with them precious thoughts of His care and love, that they may be cheered in all the employments of daily life, that they may have grace to deal honestly and faithfully in all things. We must gather about the cross. Christ and Him crucified should be the theme of contemplation, of conversation, and of our most joyful emotion. We should keep in our thoughts every blessing we receive from God, and when we realize His great love we should be willing to trust everything to the hand that was nailed to the cross for us.

It should be a pleasure to worship the Lord and to take part in His work.

The soul may ascend nearer heaven on the wings of praise. God is worshiped with song and music in the courts above, and as we express our gratitude we are approximating to the worship of the heavenly hosts. "Whoso offereth praise glorifieth" God. Psalm 50:23. Let us with reverent joy come before our Creator, with "thanksgiving, and the voice of melody." Isaiah 51:3.

WHAT TO DO WITH DOUBT

Many, especially those who are young in the Christian life, are at times troubled with the suggestions of skepticism. There are in the Bible many things which they cannot explain, or even understand, and Satan employs these to shake their faith in the Scriptures as a revelation from God. They ask, "How shall I know the right way? If the Bible is indeed the word of God, how can I be freed from these doubts and perplexities?"

God never asks us to believe, without giving sufficient evidence upon which to base our faith. His existence, His character, the truthfulness of His word, are all established by testimony that appeals to our reason; and this testimony is abundant. Yet God has never removed the possibility of doubt. Our faith must rest upon evidence, not demonstration. Those who wish to doubt will have opportunity; while those who really desire to know the truth will find plenty of evidence on which to rest their faith.

It is impossible for finite minds fully to comprehend the character or the works of the Infinite One. To the keenest intellect, the most highly educated mind, that holy Being must ever remain clothed in mystery, "Canst thou by searching find out God? canst thou find out the Almighty unto perfection? It is as high as heaven; what canst thou do? deeper than hell; what canst thou know?" Job 11:7, 8.

The apostle Paul exclaims, "O the depth of the riches both of the wisdom and knowledge of God! how unsearchable are His judgments, and His ways past finding out!" Romans 11:33. But though "clouds and darkness are round about Him," "righteousness and judgment are the foundation of His throne." Psalm 97:2, R.V. We can so far comprehend His dealings with us, and the motives by which He is actuated, that we may discern boundless love and mercy united to infinite power. We can understand as much of His purposes as it is for our good to know; and beyond this we must still trust the hand that is omnipotent, the heart that is full of love.

(35☛ The word of God, like the character of its divine Author, presents mysteries that can never be fully comprehended by finite beings. The entrance of sin into the world, the incarnation of

K N O W I N G G O D

BIRD TALK

The snowstorm caught everyone off guard. *I guess no one is going to school today*, Brian thought as he began to shovel the back sidewalk. He was surprised to hear several thumps against the back window. Snowballs? No, it was a small flock of birds, lost in the storm and searching for shelter.

They need help, Brian thought. *They'll freeze in this weather*. He opened the door of the shed and turned on the light. The birds stayed away from it. He scattered crumbs in a trail leading in. They weren't interested. Finally, he tried to drive them in. They scattered in the snow.

Don't they know I'm trying to save them? he thought. *If only I could speak their language!* He gave up and left them in the snow. *I guess the only way I could save them is if I were a bird too*, he thought.

Then it struck him. God must have felt the same way about humans.

Read the indicated paragraph (see (35☛ on page 109) to find out how much more there is to God than we can possibly imagine.

- Why would a God we can barely comprehend die for us?
- How does knowing God affect the way you live?

CONSIDER...

- watching the sunset tonight. What does it communicate about God's love for you?
- helping a child know God better. What will you say or do?

FOR MORE, SEE...

- Isaiah 1:18
- John 17:3
- Romans 8:38, 39

—JT

Christ, regeneration, the resurrection, and many other subjects presented in the Bible, are mysteries too deep for the human mind to explain, or even fully to comprehend. But we have no reason to doubt God's word because we cannot understand the mysteries of His providence. In the natural world we are constantly surrounded with mysteries that we cannot fathom. The very humblest forms of life present a problem that the wisest of philosophers is powerless to explain. Everywhere are wonders beyond our ken. Should we then be surprised to find that in the spiritual world also there are mysteries that we cannot fathom? The difficulty lies solely in the weakness and narrowness of the human mind. God has given us in the Scriptures sufficient evidence of their divine character, and we are not to doubt His word because we cannot understand all the mysteries of His providence.

The apostle Peter says that there are in Scripture "things hard to be understood, which they that are unlearned and unstable wrest . . . unto their own destruction." 2 Peter 3:16. The difficulties of Scripture have been urged by skeptics as an argument against the Bible; but so far from this, they constitute a strong evidence of its divine inspiration. If it contained no account of God but that which we could easily comprehend; if His greatness and majesty could be grasped by finite minds, then the Bible would not bear the unmistakable credentials of divine authority. The very grandeur and mystery of the themes presented should inspire faith in it as the word of God.

The Bible unfolds truth with a simplicity and a perfect adaptation to the needs and longings of the human heart, that has astonished and charmed the most highly cultivated minds, while it enables the humblest and uncultured to discern the way of salvation. And yet these simply stated truths lay hold upon subjects so elevated, so far-reaching, so infinitely beyond the power of human comprehension, that we can accept them only because God has declared them. Thus the plan of redemption is laid open to us, so that every soul may see the steps he is to take in repentance toward God and faith toward our Lord Jesus Christ, in order to be saved in God's appointed way; yet beneath these truths, so easily understood, lie mysteries that are the hiding of His glory—mysteries that overpower the mind in its research, yet inspire the sincere seeker for truth with reverence and faith. The more he searches the Bible, the deeper is his conviction that it is the word of the living God, and human reason bows before the majesty of divine revelation.

Because they cannot fathom all its mysteries, the skeptic and the infidel reject God's word.

To acknowledge that we cannot fully comprehend the great truths of the Bible is only to admit that the finite mind is inadequate to grasp the infinite; that man, with his limited, human knowledge, cannot understand the purposes of Omniscience.

Because they cannot fathom all its mysteries, the skeptic and the infidel reject God's word; and not all who profess to believe the Bible are free from danger on this point. The apostle says, "Take heed, brethren, lest there be in any of you an evil heart of unbelief, in departing from the living God." Hebrews 3:12. It is right to study closely the teachings of the Bible and to search into "the deep things of God" so far as they are revealed in Scripture. 1 Corinthians 2:10. While "the secret things belong unto the Lord our God," "those things which are revealed belong unto us." Deuteronomy 29:29. But it is Satan's work to pervert the investigative powers of the mind. A certain pride is mingled with the consideration of Bible truth, so that men feel impatient and defeated if they cannot explain every portion of Scripture to their satisfaction. It is too humiliating to them to acknowledge that they do not understand the inspired words. They are unwilling to wait patiently until God shall see fit to reveal the truth to them. They feel that their unaided human wisdom is sufficient to enable them to comprehend the Scripture, and failing to do this, they virtually deny its authority. It is true that many theories and doctrines popularly supposed to be derived from the Bible have no foundation in its teaching, and indeed are contrary to the whole tenor of inspiration. These things have been a cause of doubt and perplexity to many minds. They are not, however, chargeable to God's word, but to man's perversion of it.

God intends that even in this life the truths of His word shall be ever unfolding to His people.

If it were possible for created beings to attain to a full understanding of God and His works, then, having reached this point, there would be for them no further discovery of truth, no growth in knowledge, no further development of mind or heart. God would no longer be supreme; and man, having reached the limit of knowledge and attainment, would cease to advance. Let us thank God that it is not so. God is infinite; in Him are "all the treasures of wisdom and knowledge." Colossians 2:3. And to all eternity men may be ever searching, ever learning, and yet never exhaust the treasures of His wisdom, His goodness, and His power.

God intends that even in this life the truths of His word shall be ever unfolding to His people. There is only one way in which this knowledge can be obtained. We can attain to an understanding of God's word only through the illumination of that Spirit by which the word was given. "The things of God knoweth no man, but the Spirit of God;" "for the Spirit searcheth all things, yea, the deep things of God." 1 Corinthians 2:11, 10. And the Saviour's promise to His followers was, "When He, the Spirit of truth, is come, He will guide you into all truth. . . . For He shall receive of Mine, and shall show it unto you." John 16:13, 14.

God desires man to exercise his reasoning powers; and the study of the Bible will strengthen and elevate the mind as no other study can. Yet we are to beware of deifying reason, which is subject to the weakness and infirmity of humanity. If we would not have the Scriptures clouded to our understanding, so that the plainest truths shall not be comprehended, we must have the simplicity and faith of a little child, ready to learn, and beseeching the aid of the Holy Spirit. A sense of the power and wisdom of God, and of our inability to comprehend His greatness, should inspire us with humility, and we should open His word, as we would enter His presence, with holy awe. When we come to the Bible, reason must acknowledge an authority superior to itself, and heart and intellect must bow to the great I AM.

There are many things apparently difficult or obscure, which God will make plain and simple to those who thus seek an understanding of them. But without the guidance of the Holy Spirit we shall be continually liable to wrest the Scriptures or to misinterpret them. There is much reading of the Bible that is without profit and in many cases a positive injury. When the word of God is opened without reverence and without prayer; when the thoughts and affections are not fixed upon God, or in harmony with His will, the mind is clouded with doubts; and in the very study of the Bible, skepticism strengthens. The enemy takes control of the thoughts, and he suggests interpretations that are not correct. Whenever men are not in word and deed seeking to be in harmony with God, then, however learned they may be, they are liable to err in their understanding of Scripture, and it is not safe to trust to their explanations. Those who look to the Scriptures to find discrepancies, have not spiritual insight. With distorted vision they will see many causes for doubt and unbelief in things that are really plain and simple.

(36) Disguise it as they may, the real cause of doubt and

D O U B T

FRIENDLY DESTRUCTION

By junior high Lili and Tess shared everything from clothes to secret crushes. Then one day Tess came to school and Lili wouldn't speak to her. She spent all her time with another friend. Worse, Lili told lies about Tess and made fun of her in front of everyone. Tess cried and wrote Lili letters, demanding to know what she'd done wrong. But Lili never answered.

Halfway through high school Lili began speaking to Tess once more. Within a year they were best friends again—until one day, without warning, Lili dropped her again. She turned her back on Tess whenever she saw her. She lied about her to mutual friends. *Why is she doing this to me?* Tess wondered. *I thought we were going to be friends forever.*

When Lili finally began speaking to Tess again, Tess didn't respond. She didn't trust Lili and didn't want to be hurt again.

Doubt about a person can destroy a relationship. You don't know if you can trust them. Has hurt ever made you doubt God? God will never turn His back on you. The indicated paragraph (see (36) on page 114) suggests where doubt about God really comes from.

- When someone doubts your sincerity how does it make you feel?
- How can people's actions make us doubt God?

CONSIDER...

- thinking about God's promise to Noah in Genesis 9:13-17 the next time you see a rainbow.
- making a list of all the promises you've made recently—even the small ones. Did you keep them?

FOR MORE, SEE...

- Genesis 28:15
- Psalm 33:4
- Matthew 28:20

—LM

skepticism, in most cases, is the love of sin. The teachings and restrictions of God's word are not welcome to the proud, sin-loving heart, and those who are unwilling to obey its requirements are ready to doubt its authority. In order to arrive at truth, we must have a sincere desire to know the truth and a willingness of heart to obey it. And all who come in this spirit to the study of the Bible will find abundant evidence that it is God's word, and they may gain an understanding of its truths that will make them wise unto salvation.

Christ has said, "If any man willeth to do His will, he shall know of the teaching." John 7:17, R.V. Instead of questioning and caviling concerning that which you do not understand, give heed to the light that already shines upon you, and you will receive greater light. By the grace of Christ, perform every duty that has been made plain to your understanding, and you will be enabled to understand and perform those of which you are now in doubt.

There is an evidence that is open to all,—the most highly educated, and the most illiterate,—the evidence of experience. God invites us to prove for ourselves the reality of His word, the truth of His promises. He bids us "taste and see that the Lord is good." Psalm 34:8. Instead of depending upon the word of another, we are to taste for ourselves. He declares, "Ask, and ye shall receive." John 16:24. His promises will be fulfilled. They have never failed; they never can fail. And as we draw near to Jesus, and rejoice in the fullness of His love, our doubt and darkness will disappear in the light of His presence.

The apostle Paul says that God "hath delivered us from the power of darkness, and hath translated us into the kingdom of His dear Son." Colossians 1:13. And everyone who has passed from death unto life is able to "set to his seal that God is true." John 3:33. He can testify, "I needed help, and I found it in Jesus. Every want was supplied, the hunger of my soul was satisfied; and now the Bible is to me the revelation of Jesus Christ. Do you ask why I believe in Jesus? Because He is to me a divine Saviour. Why do I believe the Bible? Because I have found it to be the voice of God to my soul." We may have the witness in ourselves that the Bible is true, that Christ is the Son of God. We know that we are not following cunningly devised fables.

God invites us to prove for ourselves the reality of His word.

Peter exhorts his brethren to "grow in grace, and in the knowledge of our Lord and Saviour Jesus Christ." 2 Peter 3:18. When the people of God are growing in grace, they will be constantly obtaining a clearer understanding of His word. They will discern new light and beauty in its sacred truths. This has been true in the history of the church in all ages, and thus it will continue to the end. "The path of the righteous is as the light of dawn, that shineth more and more unto the perfect day." Proverbs 4:18, R.V., margin.

By faith we may look to the hereafter and grasp the pledge of God for a growth of intellect, the human faculties uniting with the divine, and every power of the soul being brought into direct contact with the Source of light. We may rejoice that all which has perplexed us in the providences of God will then be made plain, things hard to be understood will then find an explanation; and where our finite minds discovered only confusion and broken purposes, we shall see the most perfect and beautiful harmony. "Now we see through a glass, darkly; but then face to face: now I know in part; but then shall I know even as also I am known." 1 Corinthians 13:12.

REJOICING IN THE LORD

The children of God are called to be representatives of Christ, showing forth the goodness and mercy of the Lord. As Jesus has revealed to us the true character of the Father, so we are to reveal Christ to a world that does not know His tender, pitying love. "As Thou hast sent Me into the world," said Jesus, "even so have I also sent them into the world." "I in them, and Thou in Me; . . . that the world may know that Thou hast sent Me." John 17:18, 23. The apostle Paul says to the disciples of Jesus, "Ye are manifestly declared to be the epistle of Christ," "known and read of all men." 2 Corinthians 3:3, 2. In every one of His children, Jesus sends a letter to the world. If you are Christ's follower, He sends in you a letter to the family, the village, the street, where you live. Jesus, dwelling in you, desires to speak to the hearts of those who are not acquainted with Him. Perhaps they do not read the Bible, or do not hear the voice that speaks to them in its pages; they do not see the love of God through His works. But if you are a true representative of Jesus, it may be that through you they will be led to understand something of His goodness and be won to love and serve Him.

Christians are set as light bearers on the way to heaven. They are to reflect to the world the light shining upon them from Christ. Their life and character should be such that through them others will get a right conception of Christ and of His service.

If we do represent Christ, we shall make His service appear attractive, as it really is. Christians who gather up gloom and sadness to their souls, and murmur and complain, are giving to others a false representation of God and the Christian life. They give the impression that God is not pleased to have His children happy, and in this they bear false witness against our heavenly Father.

Satan is exultant when he can lead the children of God into unbelief and despondency. He delights to see us mistrusting God, doubting His willingness and power to save us. He loves to have us feel that the Lord will do us harm by His providences. It is the work of Satan to represent the Lord as lacking in compassion and pity. He misstates the truth in regard to Him. He fills the imagination with false ideas concerning God; and instead of dwelling upon the truth in regard to our heavenly Father, we too often fix our minds upon the misrepresentations of Satan and dishonor God by distrusting Him and murmuring against Him. Satan ever seeks to make the religious life one of gloom. He desires it to appear toilsome and difficult; and when the Christian presents in his own life this view of religion, he is, through his unbelief, seconding the falsehood of Satan.

(37) Many, walking along the path of life, dwell upon their mistakes and failures and disappointments, and their hearts are filled with grief and discouragement. While I was in Europe, a sister who had been doing this, and who was in deep distress, wrote to me, asking for some word of encouragement. The night after I had read her letter I dreamed that I was in a garden, and one who seemed to be the owner of the garden was conducting me through its paths. I was gathering the flowers and enjoying their fragrance, when this sister, who had been walking by my side, called my attention to some unsightly briers that were impeding her way. There she was mourning and grieving. She was not walking in the pathway, following the guide, but was walking among the briers and thorns. "Oh," she mourned, "is it not a pity that this beautiful garden is spoiled with thorns?" Then the guide said, "Let the thorns alone, for they will only wound you. Gather the roses, the lilies, and the pinks."

Have there not been some bright spots in your experience? Have you not had some precious seasons when your heart throbbed with joy in response to the Spirit of God? When you look back into the chapters of your life experience do you not find some pleasant pages? Are not God's promises, like the fragrant flowers, growing beside your path on every hand? Will you not let their beauty and sweetness fill your heart with joy?

The briers and thorns will only wound and grieve you; and if

POSITIVE THINKING

THE BIGGEST LOSER

Each year American baseball writers choose one pitcher from the National League and one from the American League to receive the prestigious Cy Young Award, named for a pitcher who won 511 games over the years 1890-1911, a record that almost certainly will never be broken. Cy Young, a fierce competitor who believed in himself, is recognized today as "the greatest pitcher who ever played."

Cy Young had another record, however, that also will surely never be broken. He *lost* 315 games! You could say he was the biggest loser who ever played baseball. If Cy Young had spent his time worrying over his many losses, he might have gotten discouraged and quit.

Do you spend time wishing you were better looking? more popular? smarter? It's much better to focus on the words written by the apostle Paul: "I can do all things through Christ which strengtheneth me" (Philippians 4:13). The indicated paragraph (see 37 on page 118) will give you some encouragement to keep your eyes on your positive points.

- Where do feelings of inferiority come from and what can you do about them?
- What should you focus on instead of your weak points?

CONSIDER...

- writing a list of your positive points and how Christ can use these to make you a successful person.
- reading a biography of someone who had disadvantages in life and still became successful. How you can profit from his or her experiences?

FOR MORE, SEE...

- Romans 8:17
- 2 Corinthians 4:15-18
- Philippians 3:13, 14

—*BC*

you gather only these things, and present them to others, are you not, besides slighting the goodness of God yourself, preventing those around you from walking in the path of life?

It is not wise to gather together all the unpleasant recollections of a past life,—its iniquities and disappointments,—to talk over them and mourn over them until we are overwhelmed with discouragement. A discouraged soul is filled with darkness, shutting out the light of God from His own soul and casting a shadow upon the pathway of others.

Thank God for the bright pictures which He has presented to us. Let us group together the blessed assurances of His love, that we may look upon them continually: The Son of God leaving His Father's throne, clothing His divinity with humanity, that He might rescue man from the power of Satan; His triumph in our behalf, opening heaven to men, revealing to human vision the presence chamber where the Deity unveils His glory; the fallen race uplifted from the pit of ruin into which sin had plunged it, and brought again into connection with the infinite God, and having endured the divine test through faith in our Redeemer, clothed in the righteousness of Christ, and exalted to His throne—these are the pictures which God would have us contemplate.

When we seem to doubt God's love and distrust His promises we dishonor Him and grieve His Holy Spirit. How would a mother feel if her children were constantly complaining of her, just as though she did not mean them well, when her whole life's effort had been to forward their interests and to give them comfort? Suppose they should doubt her love; it would break her heart. How would any parent feel to be thus treated by his children? And how can our heavenly Father regard us when we distrust His love, which has led Him to give His only-begotten Son that we might have life? The apostle writes, "He that spared not His own Son, but delivered Him up for us all, how shall He not with Him also freely give us all things?" Romans 8:32. And yet how many, by their actions, if not in word, are saying, "The Lord does not mean this for me. Perhaps He loves others, but He does not love me." All this is harming your own soul; for every word of doubt you utter is inviting Satan's temptations; it is strengthening in you the tendency to doubt, and it is grieving from you the ministering angels. When Satan tempts you, breathe not a word of doubt or darkness. If you choose to open the door to his suggestions, your mind will be filled with distrust and rebellious questioning. If you talk out your feelings, every doubt you express not only reacts upon yourself, but it is a seed that will germinate and bear fruit in the life of others, and it may be impossible to counteract the influence of your words. You yourself may be able to recover from the season of temptation and from the snare of Satan, but others who have been swayed by your influence may not be able to escape from the unbelief you have suggested. How important that we speak only those things that will give spiritual strength and life!

Angels are listening to hear what kind of report you are bearing to the world about your heavenly Master. Let your conversation be of Him who liveth to make intercession for you before the Father. When you take the hand of a friend, let praise to God be on your lips and in your heart. This will attract his thoughts to Jesus.

All have trials; griefs hard to bear, temptations hard to resist. Do not tell your troubles to your fellow mortals, but carry everything to God in prayer. Make it a rule never to utter one word of doubt or discouragement. You can do much to brighten the life of others and strengthen their efforts, by words of hope and holy cheer.

(38) There is many a brave soul sorely pressed by temptation, almost ready to faint in the conflict with self and with the powers

of evil. Do not discourage such a one in his hard struggle. Cheer him with brave, hopeful words that shall urge him on his way. Thus the light of Christ may shine from you. "None of us liveth to himself." Romans 14:7. By our unconscious influence others may be encouraged and strengthened, or they may be discouraged, and repelled from Christ and the truth.

ENCOURAGEMENT

UP A RIVER

For a humpback whale, Humphrey had a poor sense of direction. Taking a wrong turn off the Pacific Ocean, he wound up in San Francisco Bay. Then he swam out of the bay—and up a tributary river. Knowing he wouldn't survive on his present course, scientists and citizens alike tried to scare the stranded whale into retreat by banging on pipes and making loud underwater noises. But that just confused Humphrey, who swam further up the river.

Finally, someone remembered an experiment that has used recorded "whale songs" to attract other whales. Scientists got a whale song recording and played it from a boat behind Humphrey. The whale calls turned Humphrey around, and he followed the familiar voices back down the river and out into the Pacific.

When you've made a "wrong turn," what helps you most—harsh criticism or encouragement from friends? The indicated paragraph (see 38 on page 121) reinforces the importance of a *positive* influence.

- What's a "pipe-banging" response to a friend's problem? A "whale-song" response?
- What kind of unconscious influence do you have on your friends?

CONSIDER...

- searching out someone who seems to be "up a river" spiritually. How will you speak to him "in his own language"?
- copying on a small slip of paper the verse or verses from the Bible that give you the most encouragement. Keep the slip of paper in our purse or wallet, where you can refer to it whenever you're feeling the need for encouragement.

FOR MORE, SEE...

- 1 Corinthians 8:9-13
- Colossians 3:12-17
- Hebrews 10:23-25

—BK

There are many who have an erroneous idea of the life and character of Christ. They think that He was devoid of warmth and sunniness, that He was stern, severe, and joyless. In many cases the whole religious experience is colored by these gloomy views.

It is often said that Jesus wept, but that He was never known to smile. Our Saviour was indeed a Man of Sorrows, and acquainted with grief, for He opened His heart to all the woes of men. But though His life was self-denying and shadowed with pain and care, His spirit was not crushed. His countenance did not wear an expression of grief and repining, but ever one of peaceful serenity. His heart was a wellspring of life, and wherever He went He carried rest and peace, joy and gladness.

Our Saviour was deeply serious and intensely in earnest, but never gloomy or morose. The life of those who imitate Him will be full of earnest purpose; they will have a deep sense of personal responsibility. Levity will be repressed; there will be no boisterous merriment, no rude jesting; but the religion of Jesus gives peace like a river. It does not quench the light of joy; it does not restrain cheerfulness nor cloud the sunny, smiling face. Christ came not to be ministered unto but to minister; and when His love reigns in the heart, we shall follow His example.

If we keep uppermost in our minds the unkind and unjust acts of others we shall find it impossible to love them as Christ has loved us; but if our thoughts dwell upon the wondrous love and pity of Christ for us, the same spirit will flow out to others. We should love and respect one another, notwithstanding the faults and imperfections that we cannot help seeing. Humility and self-distrust should be cultivated, and a patient tenderness with the faults of others. This will kill out all narrowing selfishness and make us large-hearted and generous.

The psalmist says, "Trust in the Lord, and do good; so shalt thou dwell in the land, and verily thou shalt be fed." Psalm 37:3.

"Trust in the Lord." Each day has its burdens, its cares and perplexities; and when we meet how ready we are to talk of our difficulties and trials. So many borrowed troubles intrude, so many fears are indulged, such a weight of anxiety is expressed, that one might suppose we had no pitying, loving Saviour ready to hear all our requests and to be to us a present help in every time of need.

Some are always fearing, and borrowing trouble. Every day they are surrounded with the tokens of God's love; every day they are enjoying the bounties of His providence; but they overlook these present blessings. Their minds are continually dwelling upon something disagreeable which they fear may come; or some difficulty may really exist which, though small, blinds their eyes to the many things that demand gratitude. The difficulties they encounter, instead of driving them to God, the only source of their help, separate them from Him because they awaken unrest and repining.

Do we well to be thus unbelieving? Why should we be ungrateful and distrustful? Jesus is our friend; all heaven is interested in our welfare. We should not allow the perplexities and worries of everyday life to fret the mind and cloud the brow. If we do we shall always have something to vex and annoy. We should not indulge a solicitude that only frets and wears us, but does not help us to bear trials.

You may be perplexed in business; your prospects may grow darker and darker, and you may be threatened with loss; but do not become discouraged; cast your care upon God, and remain calm and cheerful. Pray for wisdom to manage your affairs with discretion, and thus prevent loss and disaster. Do all you can on your part to bring about favorable results. Jesus has promised His aid, but not apart from our effort. When, relying upon our Helper, you have done all you can, accept the result cheerfully.

It is not the will of God that His people should be weighed down with care. But our Lord does not deceive us. He does not say to us, "Do not fear; there are no dangers in your path." He knows there are trials and dangers, and He deals with us plainly. He does not propose to take His people out of a world of sin and evil, but He points them to a never-failing refuge. His prayer for His disciples was, "I pray not that Thou shouldest take them out of the world, but that Thou shouldest keep them from the evil." "In the world," He says, "ye shall have tribulation: but be of good cheer; I have overcome the world." John 17:15; 16:33.

(39) In His Sermon on the Mount, Christ taught His disciples precious lessons in regard to the necessity of trusting in God. These lessons were designed to encourage the children of God through all ages, and they have come down to our time full of instruction and comfort. The Saviour pointed His followers to the birds of the air as they warbled their carols of praise, unencumbered with thoughts of care, for "they sow not, neither do they reap." And yet the great Father provides for their needs. The Saviour asks, "Are ye not much better than they?" Matthew 6:26. The great Provider for man and beast opens His hand and supplies all His creatures. The birds of the air are not beneath His notice. He does not drop the food into their bills, but He makes provision for their needs. They must gather the grains He has scattered for them. They must prepare the material for their little nests. They must feed their young. They go forth singing to their labor, for "your heavenly Father feedeth them." And "are ye not much better than they?" Are not you, as intelligent, spiritual worshipers, of more value than the birds of the air? Will not the Author of our being, the Preserver of our life, the One who formed us in His own divine image, provide for our necessities if we but trust in Him?

Christ pointed His disciples to the flowers of the field, growing in rich profusion and glowing in the simple beauty which the heavenly Father had given them, as an expression of His love to man. He said, "Consider the lilies of the field, how they grow." The beauty and simplicity of these natural flowers far outrival the splendor of Solomon. The most gorgeous attire produced by the skill of art cannot bear comparison with the natural grace and radiant beauty of the flowers of God's creation. Jesus asks, "If God so clothe the grass of the field, which today is, and tomorrow is cast into the oven, shall He not much more clothe you, O ye of little faith?" Matthew 6:28, 30. If God, the divine Artist, gives to the

T R U S T

TAKING THE PLUNGE TOGETHER

Scuba diving is truly exciting. But through carelessness or accidents, this activity can turn sinister. Disorientation, entanglement, and air starvation can threaten your safety. A good diving partner is your best protection.

You have two responsibilities to your buddy: to keep problems from occurring and to help your partner overcome any problems that occur.

Planning your dive together and sticking to the plan helps keep problems to a minimum. Before you dive, you and your partner must clearly outline your course. Where will you go? What pattern will you follow, and for what distances? What will be your limits for depth, time, and air supply? Where do you intend to surface?

If you run into trouble with your equipment, you can share your partner's air supply while you ascend to the surface. This technique, called "buddy breathing," involves passing the regulator back and forth, with each diver taking two breaths. Practicing buddy breathing will build trust in your partner and prepare you for any emergency.

The indicated paragraph (see 39 on page 125) shows how God is your buddy, Someone you can count on for assistance in any situation.

- What are the advantages of having regular contact with God, instead of calling on Him only in an emergency?
- What is the essential "breath of life" God shares with us?

CONSIDER...

- making a list of other sports that require teamwork.
- reading a biography of a Christian who has put his or her trust in God.

FOR MORE, SEE...

- Psalm 22:4, 5
- Daniel 6:23
- John 14:1
- Hebrews 11:7

—*SN*

simple flowers that perish in a day their delicate and varied colors, how much greater care will He have for those who are created in His own image? This lesson of Christ's is a rebuke to the anxious thought, the perplexity and doubt, of the faithless heart.

The Lord would have all His sons and daughters happy, peaceful, and obedient. Jesus says, "My peace I give unto you: not as the world giveth, give I unto you. Let not your heart be troubled, neither let it be afraid." "These things have I spoken unto you, that My joy might remain in you, and that your joy might be full." John 14:27; 15:11.

Happiness that is sought from selfish motives, outside of the path of duty, is ill-balanced, fitful, and transitory; it passes away, and the soul is filled with loneliness and sorrow; but there is joy and satisfaction in the service of God; the Christian is not left to walk in uncertain paths; he is not left to vain regrets and disappointments. If we do not have the pleasures of this life we may still be joyful in looking to the life beyond.

But even here Christians may have the joy of communion with Christ; they may have the light of His love, the perpetual comfort of His presence. Every step in life may bring us closer to Jesus, may give us a deeper experience of His love, and may bring us one step nearer to the blessed home of peace. Then let us not cast away our confidence, but have firm assurance, firmer than ever before. "Hitherto hath the Lord helped us," and He will help us to the end. 1 Samuel 7:12. Let us look to the monumental pillars, reminders of what the Lord has done to comfort us and to save us from the hand of the destroyer. Let us keep fresh in our memory all the tender mercies that God has shown us,—the tears He has wiped away, the pains He has soothed, the anxieties removed, the fears dispelled, the wants supplied, the blessings bestowed,—thus strengthening ourselves for all that is before us through the remainder of our pilgrimage.

We cannot but look forward to new perplexities in the coming conflict, but we may look on what is past as well as on what is to come, and say, "Hitherto hath the Lord helped us." "As thy days, so shall thy strength be." Deuteronomy 33:25. The trial will not exceed the strength that shall be given us to bear it. Then let us take up our work just where we find it, believing that whatever may come, strength proportionate to the trial will be given.

And by and by the gates of heaven will be thrown open to admit God's children, and from the lips of the King of glory the benediction will fall on their ears like richest music, "Come, ye blessed of My Father, inherit the kingdom prepared for you from the foundation of the world." Matthew 25:34.

Then the redeemed will be welcomed to the home that Jesus is preparing for them. There their companions will not be the vile of earth, liars, idolaters, the impure, and unbelieving; but they will associate with those who have overcome Satan and through divine grace have formed perfect characters. Every sinful tendency, every imperfection, that afflicts them here has been removed by the blood of Christ, and the excellence and brightness of His glory, far exceeding the brightness of the sun, is imparted to them. And the moral beauty, the perfection of His character, shines through them, in worth far exceeding this outward splendor. They are without fault before the great white throne, sharing the dignity and the privileges of the angels.

In view of the glorious inheritance that may be his, "what shall a man give in exchange for his soul?" Matthew 16:26. He may be poor, yet he possesses in himself a wealth and dignity that the world could never bestow. The soul redeemed and cleansed from sin, with all its noble powers dedicated to the service of God, is of surpassing worth; and there is joy in heaven in the presence of God and the holy angels over one soul redeemed, a joy that is expressed in songs of holy triumph.